ANCIENT WORDS

Reflections on the Reliability and Proper Use of Scripture

ANCIENT WORDS

Ancient Words, Ever True?

Appealing to "authority" makes some people uncomfortable. "You just get your ideas from a book," they say, dismissively. "The Bible was only written by men."

When you think about it, though, the sum of all the knowledge we've acquired on our own amounts to very little. Most of our knowledge is not based on personal discovery, but on what someone we trusted told us.

Everything we know about the past we know in this way. Everything we know about things we've never seen—either because they are too small or they're too far away—we know by authority.

It turns out that knowing things by authority is one of the fundamental ways we know much of what we think we know. Appealing to authority is not in itself controversial. We do it all the time. Here's the real question about any appeal to authority: Can we trust it? Is our authority reliable or not?

In this essay, I'd like to answer that challenge regarding the Bible. I'd like to give evidence that the ancient words of the Bible are not just unreliable human inventions, but rather are the result of the supernatural hand of God.

Whenever I hear the opening lines of Michael W. Smith's song, "Ancient Words," I am always moved: "Holy words long preserved / for our walk in this world. / They resound with God's own heart. / Oh, let the ancient words impart."

Being aware of God while gazing on the ocean is all well and good, C.S. Lewis noted,[1] but if you want to go anywhere on that sparkling sea, you must have a map. Going somewhere with God is no different. In His case, though, the map is not made of symbols, but of words—ancient words.

Why Words?

Why any words at all, though? Isn't experience with God enough? As the songwriter says, "You ask me how I know He lives: He lives within my heart."

Experience has its place (Paul used his own dramatic Damascus Road encounter as evidence for skeptical Jews), but it also has its liabilities. Lots of people have spiritual experiences. Any Mormon can tell you of his experience with Jesus, the created spirit brother of Lucifer. Jehovah's Witnesses experience the incarnation of Michael the Archangel. New Agers experience Jesus the Ascended Hindu Master.

Each has an experience, but each can't be right. Which is the true Jesus? What objective authority separates wheat from chaff? Classically, Christians have turned to details recorded in Scripture as authoritative, objective grounds for truth. God has spoken in the ancient words of the Bible.

The Fingerprints of God

Hundreds of places in the Old Testament we find the phrase, "Thus saith the Lord," or its equivalent. The writer of Hebrews affirms, "God…spoke long ago to the fathers in the prophets in many portions and in many ways" (Heb. 1:1).

Jesus and the Apostles constantly affirm the authority of the Old Testament with the simple statement, "It is written…." The words of a text are attributed equally to the writers ("Moses said…") and to God ("God said…"). Paul reminds us that all Scripture is profitable precisely because it is "inspired" (*theopneustos*, "God-breathed"), the very counsel of God.

Of course, just claiming it's so doesn't make it so. How do we know? Do we have any evidence God has spoken in the Bible?

The challenge can be reduced to a simple question: "What kind of book is the Bible?" I submit there are only two plausible answers. *The Bible is merely a book by man about God, or it is a book given by God through man, to man.*

If the first, then the Bible is a record of human wisdom marked by human limitations. That's all.[2] If the second, then God is the ultimate author and His word is the last word. Further, being essentially a supernatural book, it would likely bear supernatural marks—God's fingerprints, in a sense.

Do we have any good reasons to think God has spoken supernaturally in the Bible? Or have men merely opined? The way to answer this question is to look at the book itself. I want to offer six reasons I think the Bible is God's book, six evidences of supernatural authorship conveniently paired with parts of the hand so you won't forget. [3]

The "Pinky"

For the first evidence, think "pinky—prophecy." The Bible has fulfilled prophecy—detailed, precise, predictions relating to individuals and entire empires given with hairsplitting accuracy.

Daniel gives prophecy so exact it reads like history written after the fact. For one, at the threshold of the fulfillment of Jeremiah's prophecy of 70 years of Babylonian captivity for Judah (Jer. 29:10), Daniel is given the amazing "70 weeks" prophecy. Identifying the specific time of Messiah's advent and subsequent execution, it was fulfilled in the exact 173,880-day time period he predicted (Daniel 9:24-25, cf., Luke 19:41-44).[4]

There were dozens of specific prophecies fulfilled in Jesus' life alone.[5] His own prediction that the temple would be destroyed stone by stone (Luke 21:5-6) was dramatically fulfilled 40 years later when Roman legions under Titus razed Jerusalem.

Is fulfilled prophecy sufficient in itself to make our case for divine authorship? Maybe not for some. Even so, it's an important piece of a cumulative case for the Scripture's divine authorship. Chalk up one for the supernatural side.

The Ring Finger

A wedding ring, symbolic of marital unity, reminds us of the second evidence for the Bible's supernatural origin—a remarkable unity of purpose and plan despite its diverse origins.

The Bible consists of sixty-six books written by forty or more authors from diverse backgrounds (rabbis, warriors, shepherds, kings, historians), in a diversity of conditions (dungeons, deserts, battlefields, palaces, pastures), on a diversity of controversial subjects, over a fifteen-hundred-year period of time.

The Bible doesn't read like sixty-six different stories, though. Instead, a profound harmony of perspective is woven through the account from Genesis to Revelation as God progressively unveils His rescue plan for fallen creation.

No individual writer understood the plan completely. Each in his time, as if guided by an unseen hand, added his piece to the puzzle. Later, at the advent of Christ, all the pieces come together, revealing the full picture of God's strategy for salvation that had been unfolding for ages.[6]

This remarkable continuity defies naturalistic explanation. Chalk up two for the supernatural side.

🏃 The Large Finger

The largest finger brings to mind the Bible's ability to address the big issues of life in a coherent way that's also entirely consistent with our deepest intuitions about reality. Simply put, the worldview of the Bible makes sense.

First, the fundamental questions vexing mankind for millennia are all confronted in Scripture: What is life's meaning? Who is God? What does He want? What makes man special? Why is there evil? What went wrong? How can we fix it?

Second, we are all intuitively aware of certain unavoidable facts. The universe is filled with order, meaning, and moral significance. Man is a unique creature, distinct from all other living things in his transcendent nobility, but is deeply damaged and morally broken, plagued by guilt he desperately tries to suppress.

The biblical worldview takes each of these things seriously. The universe is filled with order, meaning, and morality by a holy Creator who made us for friendship with Him. Yet we rebelled against our Sovereign, severing that relationship, damaging our own souls, and crippling the created order.

Evil is the wreckage left behind by our rebellion. Man is noble because he bears God's image. Man is cruel because he is fallen. He *feels* guilty because he *is* guilty. Though our hearts long for restoration, reconciliation, and forgiveness, our wills remain defiant. Only God can rescue us.

Deep inside we already know most of these things. The Bible simply connects the dots, then offers the sole solution to the central problem. The problem is personal guilt that comes with rebellion. The solution is forgiveness that comes with surrender, what the Bible calls "repentance."

The Bible has supernatural insight. Its assessment of the problem and its prescription for the cure both resonate with our deepest longings, and also fit our common-sense intuitions about the world and ourselves. Chalk up three for the supernatural side.

✒ The Index Finger

The index, or "pointing," finger reminds me that the Bible points to history for verification. It's a reliable, detailed record from the distant past of events that have profound spiritual significance. This is important for two reasons.

First, a book allegedly given by God must get its history right. And it does.[7] Menahem Mansoor, professor emeritus at the University of Wisconsin at Madison, has affirmed, "Biblical archaeology's greatest significance is that it has corroborated many historical records in the Bible."[8]

David Ussishkin, Jewish professor of archaeology at Tel Aviv University, acknowledges: "In general, the evidence of material culture fits the biblical account beginning with the period of the settlement of the tribes of Israel in the land of Canaan and the establishment of the kingdom of Israel."[9]

Archaeology and the biblical record fit hand in glove. The trade journal *Biblical Archaeological Review* demonstrates this time and again. No other religious book can summon historical evidence to support its unique theological claims.[10]

The New Testament documents are the best historical documents of the ancient world when approached using the standard canons of historical research untainted by naturalistic (anti-supernatural) presuppositions. There are five reasons historians take the New Testament material seriously.[11]

First, the accounts are early. As ancient records go, the narratives were written very close to the events they report.

Second, multiple, independent, primary source documents verify each other. In addition to the works of Matthew, Mark, Luke, John, and the writings of Peter and Paul, 17 secular references[12] along with prodigious archaeological evidence further corroborate the canonical accounts.

Third, the New Testament documents include details of eyewitness testimony: times of day, weather conditions, local customs, names of provincial rulers, and other minutia characteristic of authentic accounts.

Fourth, the Gospels include embarrassing details. Jesus' disciples are petty, slow to understand, arrogant, and unfaithful. Peter denies Christ; the rest flee. Women, disrespected in the ancient world, are the first to witness the risen Christ. Why include these unflattering details if the Gospels are works of fiction?

Fifth, there was no motivation for the writers to deceive. Those who lie do so out of self-interest. A testimony that brings torment, torture, and execution is not likely to be fabricated. The earliest disciples—those who were in a position to know the truth—signed their testimonies in blood. Peter wrote, "We did not follow cleverly devised tales when we made known to you the power and coming of our Lord Jesus Christ, but we were eyewitnesses of His majesty" (2 Pet. 1:16). His claim fits all the facts.[13]

In the most successful work of history in history, *The Story of Civilization*, Pulitzer Prize winning historian Will Durant writes:

> *Despite the prejudices and theological preconceptions of the evangelists, they record many incidents that many inventors would have concealed. No one reading these scenes can doubt the reality of the figure behind them.... After two centuries of higher criticism, the outlines of the life, character and teachings of Christ remain reasonably clear and constitute the most fascinating feature in the history of Western man.[14]*

"But isn't the Qur'an historically accurate?" I am asked. Possibly, but that alone is not adequate to show supernatural authorship. Something more is needed, which leads to the second point: Unlike the Qur'an, the Bible is a record of *supernatural* events.[15]

The historical documents of the Gospels not only record Jesus' claim to be God. They also faithfully document the miracles and resurrection from the dead that substantiate this claim. Jesus' acts of power give His words tremendous authority (John 20:30-31).

If these things really happened, then Jesus is no ordinary man, and the book He endorsed as divine is no ordinary book. History itself is our ally here.

In a dramatic reversal of New Testament scholarship over the last 50 years, the majority of scholars—even secular ones—now affirm four facts of history. One, Jesus of Nazareth died on a Roman cross and was buried in a tomb. Two, the tomb was empty Sunday morning. Three, numerous people (including skeptics like James and Saul) experienced what they thought was the resurrected Jesus. Four, belief in the resurrection launched the early church.[16]

What historians do not agree on is what best explains these four facts of history. But there aren't that many options. No explanation fits the evidence better than the one given by those previously gutless disciples who now put their lives on the line for this testimony: He who was dead is alive. He has risen.

The Bible records supernatural events in history to support its claims. Chalk up four for the supernatural side.

🐦 Thumbs Up

"Thumbs up" was the emperor's sign that a gladiator had won the right to live to fight again. It reminds me that the Bible supernaturally changes people's lives in deep, profound, and irreversible ways.

This is the acid test of God's influence on revelation, its ability to dramatically transform. Whether old or young, rich or poor, learned or illiterate, noble or of mean birth, regardless of culture or country or era, the Bible has a revolutionary impact on those who heed its counsel.

And it's promised in the text: "Therefore if anyone is in Christ, he is a new creature. The old things passed away. Behold, new things have come" (2 Cor. 5:17). When people consistently obey this book, something radical happens, both to individuals and to whole cultures.[17]

Yes, people can change on their own. However, obedience to Scripture changes us in ways we could never have accomplished by ourselves (we've tried). The Bible has a supernatural impact in human lives. Chalk up five for the supernatural side.

🐦 The Fist

The clenched fist reminds me that the Bible is a fighter. It has demonstrated remarkable survival through time and persecution.

Jesus said, "Heaven and earth shall pass away, but My words will not pass away" (Matt. 13:31). Isaiah wrote, "The grass withers, the flower fades, but the Word of our God stands forever" (Is. 40:8). In prison himself for the Bible's testimony, Paul promised, "The Word of God cannot be imprisoned" (2 Tim. 2:9).

No other book in history has seen such concerted attempts to obliterate it—both externally (through destruction) and internally (through criticism)—to no avail. No other book has been printed as much, translated as much, read as much, or quoted as much as the Bible. No other name has been written about as much, pondered as much, sung about as much, or recognized as much all over the globe as the name of Jesus.

The Bible's obituary has been written many times, but it refuses to stay in the grave. It remains today the best-selling book of all time. If this book had not been the book of God, men would have destroyed it long ago. This defies a naturalistic explanation. Chalk up six for the supernatural side.

🐾 A Verdict and a Confession

The Bible has the stamp of the supernatural: supernatural predictions, supernatural unity, supernatural insight, a reliable record of supernatural events, supernatural impact, and supernatural survival.

Does this *prove* the Bible is God's book? That depends upon what you consider proof. It's always possible to be mistaken, but I have built a cumulative case here. Our claim is reasonable. Christians *do* have compelling evidence for the divine authorship of the Bible.

But now I'm going to confess something surprising: These persuasive evidences have almost nothing to do with why so many people around the world are convinced that the words of the Bible are also God's own words. It certainly isn't why I believe.

I came to believe that the Bible was inspired the same way most Christians do. I encountered the truth firsthand and was changed. Without really being able to explain why, I knew I was hearing the words of God and not just the words of man.

Consider this question: When Jesus addressed the multitudes, did He routinely give six compelling reasons to believe His words before actually speaking them? No. He simply began to talk and people marveled, even His detractors.

Soldiers sent to arrest Jesus returned empty-handed. Why had they disobeyed orders? They had *listened*. "Never has a man spoken the way this man speaks," they said (Jn. 7:46). Jesus didn't start with reasons why people should believe His words. Instead, He let the words do the work themselves. And His words worked because they were the very words of God.

If you really want to know if the Bible is God's Word, read it. Let Jesus speak for Himself. There is a powerful role the Spirit plays that is hard to describe, and is therefore difficult to explain to others.

For one, it is personal, subjective. Two, it's non-rational. In a sense, we are not persuaded, as such. We are wooed and won over, and that's very different from weighing reasons and coming to conclusions. Note, I didn't say it was *ir*-rational, but non-rational. God uses a different means to change our minds about the Bible.

Even so, the reasons given above are still vital. Here's why: The *objective* reasons are important to show that our *subjective* confidence has not been misplaced, that what we've believed with our hearts can be confirmed with our minds. The ancients called this, "Faith seeking understanding."

When you start giving people reasons to change their minds—to believe in the Bible, for instance—their first instinct is to resist, to keep on believing what they've always believed. It's human nature.

Offering good reasons is a fine approach. I do it all the time. In this case, though, skeptics will find the reasons more compelling *if something else happens first*. It's best if they first *listen*.

If you want people to believe in the Bible, encourage them simply to listen to Jesus for a while, then have them draw their own conclusions. Most people respect Jesus. They've just never listened closely to what He's said. They've never allowed His words to have their impact.

Don't get into a tug-o-war with skeptics about inspiration. Instead, invite them to engage the ideas first, then let God do the heavy lifting for you. The truth you're defending has a life of it's own because the Spirit is in the words. Once others have listened a bit, any further reasons you give for biblical authority will have the soil they need to take root in.

If all the evidence—subjective *and* objective—shows that God has spoken in the Bible, then our appropriate response is to bend the knee. Our beliefs bow to revelation, because God Himself is the best authority to tell us what is right and true and good.

When God speaks, our opinions are silenced. The ancient words are the final word—"ancient words, ever true, changing me, changing you."

Endnotes

1. http://www.imperishableinheritance.com/2005/cs-lewis-on-the-importance-of-theology/

2. Of course, even if the Bible were entirely man-made, that wouldn't by itself undermine the Bible's message. There are millions of books not penned by inerrant hands that overflow with truth—even spiritual truth (Christian bookstores are filled with them). Though I believe in inerrancy, I don't need inerrant Scripture to substantiate Christianity. Christianity stands or falls not on inerrancy, but on facts of history pertaining to Jesus of Nazareth. If the salient events recorded in the Gospels actually happened, then the claims of Christ are fully justified and Christianity is on solid ground.

3. Some might object that proving the Bible with the Bible is circular. But this is not so in our case. If our method subtly presumed the thing we were trying to prove—the divine inspiration of the Bible—that would be circular. But it does not. Instead, we're merely looking to the text for evidence of divine authorship. This is not circular.

4. http://deeperwalk.lefora.com/2010/08/26/israels-70-years-exile-to-70th-and-final-week/#ad_not_found.

5. See, for example, *Messianic Christology—A Study of Old Testament Prophecy Concerning the First Coming of the Messiah*, by Arnold Fruchetenbaum (www.ariel.org).

6. See "The Bible: Fast Forward" CDs at str.org.

7. For more detail, see chapter titled "Archeology, the Bible, and the Leap of Faith."

8. *Biblical Archaeology Review*, May/June 1995, 29.

9. Ibid., 32.

10. This connection can be overstated. Piecing together hard data from thousands of years ago is difficult, and archaeological evidence is especially vulnerable to bias in its interpretation. Old Testament scholars of the "minimalist" school, for example, characteristically refuse to accept any biblical account without independent corroboration, a virtual impossibility when dealing with texts this ancient and not a demand made on other texts. Even so, a very strong case can be made for the correlation of biblical historical claims and archaeological evidence. An even-handed approach using the standard criteria of historiography minus naturalistic bias yields high marks for the Bible as an historical source. McDowell's *New Evidence that Demands a Verdict* (Nashville: Thomas Nelson, 1999) covers this ground thoroughly.

11. See STR's "Jesus: Man or Myth" at str.org for more detail. See also Habermas and Licona's *The Case for the Resurrection of Jesus* (Grand Rapids: Kregel, 2004), chapter 2.

12. Gary Habermas, *The Verdict of History* (Nashville: Thomas Nelson, 1988), 108.

13. See also Richard Bauckham's *Jesus and the Eyewitnesses* (Grand Rapids: Eerdmans, 2006).

14. Will Durant, *Caesar and Christ*, vol. 3 of *The Story of Civilization* (New York: Simon & Schuster, 1972), 557.

15. By the way, these are accounts, not "Bible stories." They really happened.

16. See Habermas and Licona's *The Case for the Resurrection of Jesus*, chapters 3 and 4, and William Lane Craig's *Reasonable Faith*, third edition (Wheaton: Crossway, 2008), 349, 361-389.

17. See "Christianity's Real Record" at str.org. See also Alvin Schmidt, *Under the Influence—How Christianity Transformed Civilization* (Grand Rapids: Zondervan, 2001) and Carroll and Shiflett, *Christianity on Trial* (San Francisco: Encounter Books, 2002).

Can We Trust the New Testament Documents?

The challenge regarding the reliability of the New Testament texts can be stated very simply: "The Bible has been changed and translated so many times over the last 2000 years, it's impossible to know what it originally said. Everyone knows that."

This invocation of common knowledge is enough to satisfy the ordinary, man-on-the-street critic of Christianity, and the challenge has stopped countless believers in their tracks. And the response to books like Bart Ehrman's bestseller, Misquoting Jesus, *shows the public's appetite for ammunition on this issue.*

The complaint is understandable. Whisper a message from person to person in a circle, then compare the message's final form with the original. The radical transformation in so short a period of time is enough to convince the casual skeptic that the early Christian manuscripts are equally malleable.

The question of New Testament reliability is not a religious question. It's an academic one. It can be answered in a thoughtful way by a simple appeal to facts without any reference to personal "faith" and regardless of personal spiritual convictions.

All that's needed is a simple appeal to facts. And that's what I give you in this essay.

In *Misquoting Jesus*, the *New York Times* bestseller subtitled *The Story Behind Who Changed the Bible and Why*, author Bart Ehrman fires a shot meant to sink the ship of any Christian who thinks the New Testament documents can be trusted. Here it is:

> *What good is it to say that the autographs (i.e., the originals) were inspired? We don't have the originals! We have only error-ridden copies, and the vast majority of these are centuries removed from the originals and different from them, evidently, in thousands of ways.... There are more variations among our manuscripts than there are words in the New Testament.*[1] [emphasis in the original]

Ehrman is right on the facts, as far as they go. There are 130,000 words in the New Testament, yet the surviving manuscripts (the handwritten copies) reveal something like 400,000 individual times the wording disagrees between them.[2] Indeed, Ehrman points out, the manuscripts "differ from one another in so many places that we don't even know how many differences there are."[3]

Further, Bart Ehrman is an accomplished scholar with impeccable bona fides. He co-authored *The Text of the New Testament (4th Edition)*—an academic standard in the field—with Bruce Metzger, arguably the greatest New Testament manuscript scholar alive at the time.[4]

The *Washington Post* says *Misquoting Jesus* "casts doubt on any number of New Testament episodes that most Christians take as, well gospel." *Publishers Weekly* promises that Ehrman's arguments "ensure that readers might never read the gospels or Paul's letters the same way again."[5]

Which, of course, is exactly what Ehrman wants. *Misquoting* is the kind of what-they-don't-want-you-to-know exposé that has become popular in recent years. Ehrman "exposes" discoveries that sabotaged his own "born-again" faith while a graduate student at Princeton, leaving him with the agnosticism about God he now embraces.[6]

Has the Bible been changed over 2,000 years of copying and recopying? Ehrman answers, "Yes, significantly." Worse, the massive number of alterations make it virtually impossible to have any confidence of reconstructing the autographs.

The Problem

Without the original renderings, there is no inspired text. Without inspired Scripture, there is no orthodox Christianity, only a jumble of spiritual ideas about Jesus expressed in a diverse body of conflicting texts that have tumbled down to us through the corridors of time.

Is this skepticism justified? How can we know the documents we have in our possession correctly reflect originals that disintegrated two millennia ago?

Communication is never perfect. People make mistakes. Errors are compounded with each generation. When we try to conceptualize how to reconstruct an original after thousands of years of copying, re-copying, translating, and copying some more, the task appears impossible. It's anyone's guess what the original said. Right?

Simply put, no. The skepticism is not justified once you know the facts. In spite of Ehrman's credentials, his who-knows-what-the-original-text-said view is not the majority opinion of textual scholars. This includes Bruce Metzger, Ehrman's mentor, to whom he dedicated the book. The reasons for this confidence are based on the nature of the reconstructive task itself.

A manuscript is a hand-copied text. For the first 1500 years after Christ, all copies of the Bible were reproduced by scribes who did the best they could—in most cases—to faithfully transmit the text. Inevitably, mistakes happened, which were then compounded geometrically when the flaw was copied, spawning multiple copies with the same error in subsequent generations of texts.[7] Some changes, it seems clear, were intentional and even theologically motivated, adding further complication.

Given that history, it's hard to imagine how an original can be restored after it has been handed down, copy by fragile copy, for 2000 years. The skepticism, though, is based on two misconceptions by the rank and file about the history of the communication of ancient material like that found in the New Testament.

The first assumption is that the transmission is more or less linear—one person passing the message on to a second who gives it to a third, etc., leaving a single message many generations removed from the original. Second, the objection assumes oral transmission which is more easily distorted and misconstrued than something written.

Neither assumption applies to the text of the New Testament. First, the transmission was not linear, but geometric—e.g., one letter birthed 10 copies which generated 100 and so on. Second, the transmission was done in writing, and written manuscripts can be tested in a way oral communications cannot.

🦎 Reconstructing Aunt Sally's Recipe

Let me illustrate how such a test can be made. It will help you see how scholars confidently reconstruct an original from conflicting manuscripts that are centuries removed from the autograph.

Pretend your Aunt Sally learns in a dream the recipe for an elixir that preserves her youth. When she awakes, she carefully records the complex directions on a sheet of paper, then runs to the kitchen to mix up her first batch. In a few days, she is transformed into a picture of radiant youth from her daily dose of what comes to be known as "Aunt Sally's Secret Sauce."

Aunt Sally is so excited she sends detailed, handwritten instructions to her three bridge partners (Aunt Sally is still in the technological dark ages—no photocopier or email). They, in turn, make copies for ten of their own friends.

All goes well until one day Aunt Sally's schnauzer eats the original copy of the recipe. In a panic she contacts her friends who have mysteriously suffered similar mishaps. The alarm goes out to the others who received copies from her card-playing trio in an attempt to recover the original wording.

Sally rounds up all the surviving handwritten copies, 26 in all. When she spreads them out on the kitchen table, she immediately notices some differences. Twenty-three of the copies are virtually the same save for misspelled words and abbreviations littering the text. Of the remaining three, however, one lists some ingredients in a different order, another has two phrases inverted ("mix then chop" instead of "chop then mix"), and one includes an ingredient not mentioned in any other list.

Here is the critical question: Do you think Aunt Sally could accurately reconstruct her original recipe from this evidence? Of course she could. The misspellings and abbreviations are inconsequential, as is the order of ingredients in the list (those variations all *mean* the same thing). The single inverted phrase stands out and can easily be repaired because one can't mix something that hasn't been chopped first. Sally would then simply strike the extra ingredient, reasoning it's more plausible one person would mistakenly add an item than 25 people would accidentally omit it.

Even if the variations were more numerous and diverse, the original could still be reconstructed with a high level of confidence with enough copies and a little common sense.

This, in simplified form (very simplified, but you get the point), is how scholars do "textual criticism," an academic enterprise used to reconstitute all documents of antiquity—not just religious texts—when the original has not survived. This includes historical and literary writings.

Textual criticism is not a haphazard effort based on guesses, hopes, and leaps of religious faith. It is a careful, analytical process governed by a set of established rules. It allows a trained scholar to determine the extent of possible corruption of a work and, given certain conditions, reconstruct the autograph/original with a high degree of certainty, even with many generations intervening.

This last point raises the key question of this entire discussion: *Regardless of the raw number of variants, can we recover the original reading with confidence?* The answer to that pivotal question depends on three factors.

First, how many copies exist to examine and compare? Are there two copies? ten? a hundred? The more copies there are, the easier it is to make meaningful comparisons. Second, how old are the manuscripts? How close in time are the oldest existing documents to the original? Third, what is the exact nature of the differences (the variants)?

How Many and How Old?

If the number of manuscripts available for comparison are few and the time gap between the original and the oldest copy is wide, then the autograph is harder to reconstruct with confidence. However, if there are many copies and the oldest existing ones are reasonably close in time to the original, the scholar can be more certain she has pinpointed the exact wording of the initial text, for all practical purposes.[8]

To get an idea of the significance of the volume of New Testament manuscript evidence, note for a moment the record for non-biblical texts. These are secular writings historians rely on for all their data from antiquity that have been restored with a high level of confidence based on available textual evidence— existing numbers of ancient copies.[9]

The important first century document *The Jewish War*, by Jewish aristocrat and historian Josephus, survives in only nine complete manuscripts dating from the 5th century—four centuries after it was written.[10] Tacitus' *Annals of Imperial Rome* is one of the chief historical sources for the Roman world of New Testament times, yet, surprisingly, it survives in only two manuscripts dating from the Middle Ages.[11] Thucydides' *History* survives in eight copies. There are ten copies of Caesar's *Gallic Wars*, eight copies of Herodotus' *History*, and seven copies of Plato, all dated over a millennium from the original. Homer's *Iliad* has the most impressive manuscript evidence for any secular work with 647 existing copies.[12]

For most ancient documents only a handful of manuscripts exist, some facing a time gap of 800-1500 years or more. Yet scholars are confident they have reconstructed the originals with a high degree of accuracy. In fact, virtually all of our knowledge of ancient history depends on documents like these.

New Testament expert F.F. Bruce puts the discussion in perspective: "No classical scholar would listen to an argument that the authenticity of Herodotus or Thucydides is in doubt because the earliest manuscripts of their works which are of any use to us are over 1300 years later than the originals."[13]

The Biblical Manuscript Evidence

The evidence for the New Testament is stunning by comparison. A recent count shows 5,500 separate Greek manuscripts.[14] These are represented by early fragments, uncial codices (multiple books of the New Testament written with capital Greek letters and bound together in book form), and minuscules (texts written in cursive style with small Greek letters).

Among the 2,795 minuscule fragments dating from the 9th to the 15th centuries there are 34 complete New Testaments.[15] Uncial manuscripts providing virtually complete codices date back to the 4th century. The nearly complete Codex Vaticanus is likely the oldest, dated c. 325-350.[16] The magnificent Codex Sinaiticus, purchased by the British government from the Soviet government at Christmas, 1933, for £100,000,[17] is dated c. 340.[18] It contains half the Old Testament and virtually all of the New Testament. Codex Alexandrinus contains the whole Old Testament and a nearly complete New Testament and dates from the mid-5th century.[19]

The most fascinating evidence comes from the fragments (as opposed to the codices). The Chester Beatty Papyri contains most of the New Testament and is dated mid-third century.[20] The Bodmer Papyri II collection, whose discovery was announced in 1956, includes most of the first fourteen chapters of the Gospel of

John and much of the last seven chapters. It dates from A.D. 200 or earlier.[21]

The most amazing find of all, however, is a small portion of John 18:31-33 discovered in Egypt. Known as the John Rylands Papyri and barely three inches square, it represents the earliest verified copy of any part of the New Testament. The papyri is dated on paleographical grounds at A.D. 117-138 (though it may even be earlier),[22] showing that the Gospel of John was circulated as far away as Egypt within 40 years of its composition.

Keep in mind that most papyri are fragmentary. Only about 50 manuscripts contain the entire New Testament. Even so, the textual evidence is exceedingly rich, especially when compared to other works of antiquity.

Two other cross-checks on the accuracy of the manuscripts remain: ancient versions (translations) and citations by early church Fathers known as "patristic quotations."

Early in the history of the Church, the Scriptures were translated into Latin (10,000 copies exist[23]). By the 3rd and 4th centuries the New Testament had been translated and reproduced in Coptic and Syriac, and soon after in Armenian and Georgian, among others.[24] These ancient versions were a great aid to missionaries reaching new cultures in their own language as the Gospel spread and the church grew. Translations serve as cross-checks, helping modern-day scholars answer questions about the underlying Greek manuscripts.

In addition, there are ancient extra-biblical sources—catechisms, lectionaries, and quotes from the church fathers—that cite Scripture at great length. Paul Barnett makes note of the near avalanche of early Christian books produced in the first few centuries: "Scriptures... gave rise to an immense output of early Christian literature which quoted them at length and, in effect, preserved them."[25] Indeed, the patristic (church fathers) quotations themselves include virtually every New Testament verse.[26]

I want you to notice something here. The chief concern Bart Ehrman raises regarding the biblical texts—the massive number of variants—can only arise with a massive number of manuscripts. Scholars universally consider this a virtue, not a vice—good news, not bad—because the condition causing the problem is the very condition providing the solution. The more manuscripts available for comparison, the more changes that will likely appear, but also the more raw material to use for comparison to fix the problem the variants pose.

This mountain of manuscripts gives us every reason to believe the originals have been preserved in the aggregate. No missing parts need be replaced. We have 110% of the text, not 90%.[27] The real question is this: Do we know how to separate the wheat from the chaff to recover the original reading? That depends entirely on our last question: What is the nature of the variants themselves?

✍ Those Pesky Variants

According to manuscript expert Daniel Wallace, "A textual variant is simply any difference from a standard text (e.g., a printed text, a particular manuscript, etc.) that involves spelling, word order, omission, addition, substitution, or a total rewrite of the text."[28] Note that *any* difference, no matter how slight, is added to the total count.

What exactly are those differences? They can be divided into two categories: significant variants and insignificant ones. An insignificant variant has absolutely no bearing on our ability to reconstruct the original text. The *meaning* remains the same, regardless of which *reading* is the original.

For example, well over half the variants (yes, more than 200,000) are spelling errors,[29] due either to accident (the ie/ei mistake is as common in Scripture as it is in our own writing), or different choices of phonetic spelling (*kreinai* vs. *krinai*). A host of others are immaterial differences in abbreviation or style (a definite article appearing before a name—"the James"—omitted in another because it adds nothing to the meaning).[30]

Clearly, some variations that are *textually* insignificant are *theologically* important. The rendering in the King James Version of 1 John 5 (the infamous *Comma Johanneum*) appearing to echo the Trinity *is* about a significant doctrinal issue, but clearly this variant is not in the original so it creates no textual concern. It appears in only four manuscripts, the earliest dating from the 10th century (four others have it penciled into the margin by a scribe),[31] and is almost universally acknowledged to be a corruption. Further, the doctrine of the Trinity does not rely on this text, but is verified by many other passages not in question.

A similar problem occurs with thousands of other variants that appear in only one manuscript (called "singular readings"). These obvious mistakes are easily corrected.

Here's how Wallace sums up the variations: [32]

1. Spelling differences or nonsense readings (e.g., a skipped line)
2. Inconsequential word order ("Christ Jesus" vs. "Jesus Christ") and synonyms
3. Textually meaningful, though non-viable variants (e.g., the Comma Johanneum)
4. Variants that are both meaningful and viable

Wallace's last category—the only one that matters for accurately restoring the text—constitutes "much less than" 1% of all variations.[33] In other words, *more than 396,000 of the variants have no bearing on our ability to reconstruct the original.* Even with the *textually* viable differences that remain, the vast majority are so *theologically* insignificant they are "relatively boring."[34] These facts Ehrman himself freely admits:

> *Most of the changes found in our early Christian manuscripts have nothing to do with theology or ideology. Far and away the most changes are the result of mistakes, pure and simple—slips of the pen, accidental omissions, inadvertent additions, misspelled words, blunders of one sort of another.*[35]

Wallace's fourth category—those variants both *meaningful and viable* (in a textual sense)—is the only one of any consequence. "We are talking here," write Kostenberger and Kruger, "about a situation where there are two (or more) possible readings, and the evidence for each reading...is relatively equal."[36]

Here the analytical skills of the professional textual critic are applied to weed out the most unlikely variants. She has at her disposal a specific set of rules—the accepted canons of textual analysis—that enable her to resolve the vast majority of conflicts and recover the original with a high degree of confidence.

Ironically, this is precisely the point Ehrman unwittingly demonstrates as he closes out his case against the New Testament documents.

✤ Ehrman's "Top Ten"

On the final page of the paperback edition of *Misquoting Jesus*, Ehrman lists the "Top Ten Verses That Were Not Originally in the New Testament." It serves as his parting salvo, but in reality proves his entire thesis false.

First, I immediately recognized six of the ten citations, and in every case my own Bible translation (NASB) makes a marginal note that these verses are not in the earliest manuscripts. No surprises here.

Second, one third of Ehrman's "Top Ten" list *actually is in the New Testament*, after all. Luke 22:20, 24:12, and 24:51b are, in fact, questionable *in Luke*. They do appear, however, almost word for word in uncontested passages (respectively, Matt. 26:28 and Mark 14:24; John 20:3-7; Acts 1:9, 11).

Third, nothing of theological consequence is lost by striking any of the variants that Ehrman lists, even the long ending in Mark (16:9-20) or the engaging but likely non-canonical account of Jesus and the woman caught in adultery (John 7:53-8:11).

Finally (and most damaging), Ehrman's list proves just the opposite of what he intends. For all his hand-wringing that the original text is lost forever, his list itself demonstrates it's possible to recognize the most important spurious renderings and eliminate them.

Ehrman's own works (*Misquoting Jesus* and also *The Orthodox Corruption of Scripture*) prove that the text-critical methods mentioned above—the very methods he uses to critique the New Testament—are adequate to restore the original reading. It is proof that the massive number of variants do not interfere with our ability to recapture the original, but instead the rich manuscript evidence we possess allows us to weed out the vast percentage of variants. Otherwise Ehrman would not be able to say with confidence his "Top Ten"—or any other verses—are not in the New Testament.

This is a fact he acknowledges (again, ironically) in another work. Compare the pessimism of *Misquoting Jesus* with the optimism expressed in Metzger and Ehrman's *The Text of the New Testament*:[37]

Besides textual evidence derived from New Testament

Greek manuscripts and from early versions, the textual critic compares numerous scriptural quotations used in commentaries, sermons, and other treatises written by early church fathers. Indeed, so extensive are these citations that if all other sources for our knowledge of the text of the New Testament were destroyed, they would be sufficient alone *for the reconstruction of practically the* entire New Testament. [emphasis added]

Bart Ehrman has two books with his name on them that give the exact opposite impression, and both were published the same year (2005).[38]

✿ The Final Word

What can we conclude from the evidence? Virtually all of the 400,000 differences in the New Testament documents—spelling errors, inverted words, non-viable variants and the like—are completely inconsequential to the task of reconstructing the original. Indeed, Daniel Wallace notes that a side-by-side comparison between the two main text families (the Majority Text and the modern critical text) shows agreement a full 98% of the time.[39]

Of the remaining differences, virtually all yield to a vigorous application of the accepted rules of textual criticism. This means that our New Testament is over 99% pure. In the entire text of 20,000 lines, only 40 lines are in doubt (about 400 words),[40] and none affects any significant doctrine.

Scholar D.A. Carson sums it up this way: "What is at stake is a purity of text of such a substantial nature that nothing we believe to be doctrinally true, and nothing we are commanded to do, is in any way jeopardized by the variants."[41]

This issue has long been settled in the minds of most scholars, even non-Christian ones (with the exception, recently, of Ehrman), for good reason. Simply put, if we reject the authenticity of the New Testament on textual grounds, we'd have to reject every ancient work of antiquity and declare null and void every piece of historical information from written sources prior to the beginning of the second millennium A.D.

Our chief question has been, "Can we reproduce the original New Testament to a high degree of certainty?" Even naysayer Bart Ehrman, in spite of himself, demonstrates we can.

Contrary to popular notions, even after 2000 years of recopying and translating, there is no evidence the New Testament has been corrupted. Can we know with confidence that these ancient manuscripts have been handed down accurately? Careful, critical, academic analysis says, "Yes, we can."

Endnotes

1. Bart Ehrman, *Misquoting Jesus—The Story Behind Who Changed the Bible and Why*, first paperback edition (San Francisco: HarperSanFrancisco, 2007), 7, 90.

2. Daniel Wallace, "The Number of Textual Variants: An Evangelical Miscalculation," bible.org (http://bible.org/article/number-textual-variants-evangelical-miscalculation).

3. Ehrman, 10.

4. Bruce Metzger passed away in 2007.

5. Both quotes can be found on the back cover of *Misquoting Jesus.*

6. Ehrman, 7, 257.

7. When a large number of manuscripts exhibit the same "signature" pattern of variations, they are referred to as a text family or a "text type," e.g., the Alexandrian Text, the Western Text, or the Majority Text (aka the Byzantine Text, the underlying manuscript family of the King James Version).

8. Kostenberger and Kruger, *The Heresy of Orthodoxy* (Wheaton, IL: Crossway, 2010), 205. *Sufficient* certainty is the goal, not *absolute* certainty.

9. Very minor differences in number appear in various catalogs of these documents, but these are accurate enough to make our point.

10. Paul Barnett, *Is the New Testament History?* (Ann Arbor: Vine Books, 1986), 45.

11. Geisler and Nix, *A General Introduction to the Bible* (Chicago: Moody Press, 1986), 405.

12. Bruce Metzger, *The Text of the New Testament* (New York and Oxford: Oxford University Press, 1968), 34. This number consists of 457 papyri, 2 uncials, and 188 minuscule manuscripts. More copies of Homer's work have surfaced since Metzger's count cited here.

13. F.F. Bruce, *The New Testament Documents: Are They Reliable?* (Grand Rapids: Eerdmans, 1974), 16-17.

14. Kostenberger and Kruger, 207. The number of manuscripts is continually increasing as more are discovered.

15. Geisler & Nix, 402.

16. Ibid., 391.

17. Metzger, 45.

18. Geisler & Nix, 392.

19. Ibid., 394. Visit London and you can view both of these gems—Sinaiticus and Alexandrinus—resting side by side under glass in the British Library.

20. Ibid., 389-390.

21. Metzger, 39-40.

22. Geisler and Nix, 388.

23. Kostenberger and Kruger, 208.

24. Barnett, 44.

25. Ibid., 46-47.

26. Metzger, 86.

27. Daniel Wallace, "The Majority Text and the Original Text: Are They Identical?," *Bibliotheca Sacra*, April-June, 1991, 169.

28. Daniel Wallace, "The Number of Textual Variants: An Evangelical Miscalculation" (see above).

29. Daniel Wallace, "Is What We Have Now What They Wrote Then?," http://bible.org/article/what-we-have-now-what-they-wrote-then.

30. Kostenberger and Kruger, 215-217.

31. Ibid., 219.

32. Daniel Wallace, "Is What We Have Now What They Wrote Then?" (see above)

33. Ibid.

34. Kostenberger and Kruger, 226.

35. Ehrman, 55.

36. Kostenberger and Kruger, 225.

37. Metzger and Ehrman, *The Text of the New Testament: Its Transmission, Corruption, and Restoration*, 4th Edition (New York: Oxford University Press, 2005), 126.

38. To be fair, this portion was undoubtedly authored by Metzger. Nonetheless, the ironic conflict remains.

39. Wallace, Daniel, "The Majority Text and the Original Text: Are They Identical?," 157-8. (see above)

40. Geisler and Nix, 475.

41. D.A. Carson, *The King James Version Debate* (Grand Rapids: Baker, 1979), 56.

The Da Vinci Code Cracks

"Everyone loves a conspiracy," reflected Robert Langdon, Harvard Religious Symbologist and central character in The Da Vinci Code.

Langdon's insight is key to understanding the run-away popularity of Dan Brown's blockbuster book and movie. There seems to be no end of bestsellers fueled by fertile imaginations and questionable scholarship bent on exposing "the real story" behind the myth of Christianity.

According to The Da Vinci Code, *the Bible as we know it today along with Jesus' divinity were both fabricated at the Council of Nicaea in 325 A.D. for political reasons. The authentic accounts of Jesus—depicting the Nazarene as a mere mortal who married Mary Magdalene and raised a family—were destroyed.*

This may be good fiction, but it is not serious scholarship. Brown's claims are compelling when wrapped up in energetic narrative, but on closer inspection they unravel. As it turns out, there is not a shred of reliable evidence for these charges.

What did early Christians really believe before Nicaea? We know because we have thousands of pages of their writings. In this essay I cite them, summarize them, and show you where you can easily find them for yourself.

I never thought it would happen. There I was, at a dead standstill in the middle of the 405 in Los Angeles traffic, and I didn't care. The gridlock could continue all day as far as I was concerned.

I wasn't complaining. I wasn't fidgeting. I wasn't even paying attention. Instead, I was riveted to the words flowing from my in-dash CD player. A talented reader was keeping me spellbound with a tale of murder, suspense, intrigue, and cover-up.

The story I was gripped by was *The Da Vinci Code*.

I am not alone. More than 50 million copies of Dan Brown's thriller have kept the midnight oil burning around the world. And those were of the hardbound edition. The soft cover came out with an initial release of five million. And then there's the movie.

No question about it, *The Da Vinci Code* is a blockbuster hit whose short-term publishing success is up there with the Bible. Which is ironic. Dan Brown's tale is a frontal assault on the Jesus of Christianity that millions have placed their simple trust in for 2000 years.

Brown dishes up a convoluted conspiracy of corrupted Gospels, doctrinal deception, theological suppression, book burning, the Holy Grail and, climactically, Jesus' secret marriage to Mary Magdalene whose progeny remain to this day. The Vatican lurks in the shadows, of course—maneuvering, manipulating, even murdering—suppressing the real truth for two millennia.

Jesus Gets an Upgrade

According to Brown, the epicenter of the massive deception foisted on Christians the world over is the Council of Nicaea, which met in 325 A.D. at the behest of emperor Constantine the Great. From this meeting "sprang the most profound moment in Christian history."

Here are the "facts" related to us through Dan Brown's character, the historian Sir Leigh Teabing:

> "The Bible is a product of *man*, my dear. Not of God. The Bible did not fall magically from the clouds. Man created it as a historical record of tumultuous times, and it has evolved through countless translations, additions, and revisions. History has never had a definitive version of the book...

> "[Jesus'] life was recorded by thousands of followers across the land....More than *eighty* gospels were considered for the New Testament, and yet only a relative few were chosen for inclusion—Matthew, Mark, Luke, and John among them."

> "Who chose which gospels to include?" Sophie asked.

> "Aha!" Teabing burst in with enthusiasm. "The fundamental irony of Christianity! The Bible, as we know it today, was collated by the pagan Roman emperor Constantine the Great....

> "Constantine needed to strengthen the new Christian tradition, and held a famous ecumenical gathering known as the Council of Nicaea."

Sophie had heard of it only insofar as its being the birthplace of the Nicene Creed.

"At this gathering," Teabing said, "many aspects of Christianity were debated and voted upon—the date of Easter, the role of the bishops, the administration of sacraments, and, of course the *divinity* of Christ."

"I don't follow. His divinity?"

"My dear," Teabing declared, "until *that* moment in history, Jesus was viewed by His followers as a mortal prophet…a great and powerful man, but a *man* nonetheless. A mortal."

"Not the Son of God?"

"Right," Teabing said. "Jesus' establishment as 'the son of God' was officially proposed and voted on by the Council of Nicaea."

"Hold on. You're saying Jesus' divinity was the result of a *vote*?"

"A relatively close vote at that," Teabing added….

"And I assume devout Christians send you hate mail on a daily basis?"

"Why would they?" Teabing countered. "The vast majority of educated Christians know the history of their faith…."

"The twist is this," Teabing said, talking faster now. "Because Constantine upgraded Jesus' status almost four centuries *after* Jesus' death, thousands of documents already existed chronicling His life as a *mortal* man. To rewrite the history books, Constantine knew he would need a bold stroke. From this sprang the most profound moment in Christian history." Teabing paused, eyeing Sophie. "Constantine commissioned and financed a new Bible, which omitted those gospels that spoke of Christ's *human* traits and embellished those gospels that made Him godlike. The earlier gospels were outlawed, gathered up, and burned.

"Fortunately for historians," Teabing said, "some of the gospels that Constantine attempted to eradicate managed to survive. The Dead Sea Scrolls were found in the 1950s in a cave near Qumran in the Judean desert. And, of course, the Coptic Scrolls in 1945 at Nag Hammadi….

The scrolls highlight glaring historical discrepancies and fabrications, clearly confirming that the modern Bible was compiled and edited by men who possessed a political agenda—to promote the divinity of the man Jesus Christ and use His influence to solidify their own power base." (231-234)

Though this is a work of fiction, Teabing's testimony has rocked the confidence of many Christians. It's understandable. There is an implicit trust relationship between writers of historical fiction and their readers. Readers expect an imaginary tale, but they trust the background information to be accurate. They count on the author to do his homework.

Brown invites that trust. An alert placed just before the Prologue under the bolded heading "FACT" reads, "All descriptions of artwork, architecture, documents, and secret rituals in this novel are accurate."

It's no wonder Christians are shaken. Teabing's account is so lucid, so compelling, so convincingly told. The more controversial details are characterized as the common knowledge of insiders, academics, historians, and intellectuals in general. Only the foolish faithful are still in the dark, unwitting dupes of Constantine and the Vatican.

Broken Trust

Dan Brown has betrayed our trust, though. For alert readers, this is obvious even before second-checking the details.

Consider Brown's claim, for example, that Jesus' life "was recorded by thousands," with more than eighty gospels being freely circulated for hundreds of years. If this were true, think of the herculean task facing poor Constantine. To pull off his deception, he must hunt down and destroy a mountain of manuscript copies of the authentic Jesus-is-just-a-mortal-man gospels that had been circulating throughout the Roman empire for nearly three centuries.

With all the conveniences of modern technology at my disposal, I couldn't do that with yesterday's L.A. Times circulating just in Orange County. How could Constantine's minions do it by hand on foot over the entire civilized world of that time? Previous Roman rulers—Diocletian in 303 and Maximian in 304—had tried.[1]

Problems like these are obvious on first glance. After a little sleuthing, however, more glaring discrepancies surface.

Brown claims Constantine's book-burning wasn't completely successful, that the famous Dead Sea Scrolls found in caves in Qumran "highlight glaring historical discrepancies and fabrications, clearly confirming that the modern Bible was compiled and edited by men who possessed a political agenda—to promote the divinity of the man Jesus Christ."

However, there is no mention of Jesus of Nazareth anywhere in the Dead Sea Scrolls. Qumran produced no gospels of the life of Christ of any kind. This claim is a complete invention by Dan Brown.

🏃 The Council of Nicaea

A full accounting of the misinformation, falsehoods, inventions, and distortions littering Brown's fiction is not possible here. I am not concerned now with Brown's fanciful conspiracy tales of the Holy Grail, Mary Magdalene's alleged marriage to Jesus, nor with the secret identity of His progeny living now in Paris under cover and out of reach of the Vatican. Another issue is more foundational.

None of those claims can be taken seriously unless Brown first undermines the historical legitimacy of the canonical Gospels: Matthew, Mark, Luke, and John. Only then can his revisionist history get into play.

Sir Teabing is Brown's mouthpiece for this effort. Teabing claims these records were tampered with by Constantine at the Council of Nicaea. To advance his own political agenda, the Roman emperor rewrote history, destroying the true records that cast Jesus as a mere mortal and replacing them with documents that advanced the man of Nazareth as the divine Son of God.

Since this is the pivot upon which Brown's entire yarn spins, it's vital to ask, "What really happened at Nicaea?"

If you want to know the true details of any event, it's best to consult those who were actually there. Eusebius of Caesarea and Athanasius, archdeacon of Alexandria, both wrote extensively about the controversy. Eusebius was also a central figure of the theological debate, along with the presbyter Arius and the bishop Alexander, both of Alexandria.

The basic facts are these.[2] Emperor Constantine called the Council to order and presided over it from June 14 to July 25, 325 A.D. 318 bishops attended along with two presbyters each. Three main points were discussed: the Easter question, the Meletian schism, and the divinity of Christ. Since this last issue was the precipitating reason *for* convening the council in the first place, it could hardly have been fabricated *by* the Council, as Teabing asserts.

In fact, *no one* in attendance at Nicaea, including the Arians, regarded Jesus as a "mere mortal" rather than the Son of God, however variously they may have understood that phrase's meaning. Arius denied the full deity of Christ, true enough, but he didn't think Jesus was just a man. Rather, he argued, Jesus was a unique creature, a human body with no rational human soul. Instead, He was indwelled by a created, pre-incarnate spirit called the Logos. Ironically for Brown, then, the dissenting party led by Arius denied both the deity *and* the true humanity of Christ.

A vigorous debate followed, along with failed attempts at compromise offered by Eusebius. When the ballots were finally cast, it was not a "relatively close vote," but a landslide for the orthodox party. 316 held for the deity of Christ, while two bishops from Egypt—Theonas and Secundus—dissented. By virtual unanimous consent, the council affirmed the ancient confession, Jesus is the Son of God.

Surprisingly, even the early heretics agreed on this score.

The Heretics Speak

The first great doctrinal challenge to the church in the Roman Empire was Gnosticism. It existed in seminal form in the 1st century. In the 2nd century, though, it became a full-blown competitor with apostolic Christianity.

Though Gnosticism was a complex mixture of beliefs, at its core was a radical dualism between spirit and matter in which matter was inherently evil and spirit inherently good.

For the "Christian" forms of Gnosticism, then, it was unthinkable that Christ could have been sullied with a real physical body. Instead, some claimed, He only *appeared* embodied, giving rise to a heresy called Docetism (from the Greek *dokeo*, "to appear" or "seem").

This raised problems for the incarnation. Note John's warning in the face of the growing tendency to deny Jesus' humanity: "Beloved, do not believe every spirit, but test the spirits to see whether they are from God." What was the test? "By this you know the Spirit of God: Every spirit that confesses that Jesus Christ has *come in the flesh* is from God" (1 John 4:1-2). Early on, belief in a genuine incarnation was a test of orthodoxy. Mere appearances wouldn't do.

Here's the important point: Gnosticism *affirmed* that Jesus was divine. It fell afoul of Christianity in its denial of Jesus' true human mortality, not His divine nature. This proves that Jesus' divinity was not an invention of Constantine in the 4th century.

Even more damaging for Dan Brown, the vast majority of so-called "lost" gospels (particularly those from Nag Hammadi) were Gnostic in nature. Any unqualified appeal by Brown to Gnostic writings, then, is self-defeating. Gnostics would not affirm, even in principle, that Jesus was "a mortal prophet...a great and powerful man, but a *man* nonetheless."

Modalism surfaced next. Modalists insisted Jesus was God, but denied any real distinction between the divine persons. Rather, Jesus was one mode of manifestation of God. In the Old Testament God revealed Himself in the mode of Father, in the New Testament as Son, and since Pentecost as the Holy Spirit.

The testimony of the heretics is an embarrassment for Brown. Both of these early heresies, in play for more than a 100 years before the reign of Constantine, affirmed the full divinity of Jesus of Nazareth. On this point they mimicked orthodoxy. They were condemned as heresies for other reasons. This is exactly the *opposite* of what you'd expect if Brown's assertions were correct.

But there's more:

- The book of Romans, an uncontested Pauline epistle written c. 55 A.D., shows that the claim of Jesus' divinity was circulating within 20 years of the crucifixion. Note the opening: "...declared *the Son of God* with power by the resurrection from the dead, according to the Spirit of holiness, Jesus Christ our Lord."—Romans 1:4

- Ignatius (AD 110-130) affirms Jesus as God: "We also have a Physician *the Lord our God, Jesus the Christ, the only-begotten Son and Word before time began*, but who afterwards became also man of Mary the virgin."—*The Epistle of Ignatius to the Ephesians*

- Irenaeus (AD 115-190) writes: "...in order that through *Christ Jesus, our Lord, and God*, and Savior, and King, according to the will of the invisible Father, 'every knee should bow'..."—*Against Heresies* X.1

- Justin Martyr (A.D. 110-165) writes: "In these books, then, of the prophets we found Jesus our Christ foretold as coming, born of a virgin...and *being called the Son of God.*" —*The First Apology of Justin*, XXXI

The ancient documents—available for anyone to read—speak clearly on this issue. The notion of Christ's divine nature was not "officially proposed" by the Council of Nicaea. Rather, for three centuries before Constantine, massive numbers of early followers of Christ—both inside of orthodoxy and out—believed Jesus was the Son of God.

Constantine's Great Deception?

Brown is mistaken on still another claim. He asserts, "The Bible, as we know it today, was collated by the pagan Roman Emperor Constantine the Great." This is a remarkable statement because the canon of Scripture *was never at issue at Nicaea,* for good reason. For all practical purposes, the legitimacy of the four standard gospels had been decided long before.[3]

The *formal* concept of New Testament canon did not develop until the 2nd century. Early on, though, there was an *implicit* canon: the authoritative "rule" (i.e., "canon") of the teaching of either the Apostles commissioned directly by Christ. When the last apostle died, the emphasis naturally shifted to the written record of their instruction—the Gospels and letters (epistles) they had left behind—or of those who were companions of apostles and wrote under their authority and tutelage (e.g., John Mark, companion of Peter and author of the Gospel of Mark, or Luke, the companion of Paul). Therefore, the preeminent question about any work was: Did the writing have apostolic authority?

Controversy on the canon was fueled by a Gnostic named Marcion (c. 150 A.D.) who flatly rejected, for theological reasons, works that until then had been accepted as authentic for nearly a century.

In the debate that ensued, [4] the early church identified three categories of text. The "Homologumena" consisted of those books that received unanimous support by all church leadership. This included 20 of the 27 New Testament books, *including all four Gospels*.

The "Antilegomena" were those contested. They received support from some members of church leadership, but not others. Some were ultimately rejected (Shepherd of Hermas, the Didache, Epistle of Polycarp to the Philippians, the Second Epistle of Clement). Others were ultimately accepted (Revelation, Jude, James, Hebrews, 2 Peter, 2 and 3 John).

The final group—called variously the Pseudepigrapha, Apocrypha, or simply the "heretical books"—were "set aside as altogether worthless and impious," according to Eusebius. These included hundreds of documents that received no support from the early Christians and were considered completely spurious by all orthodox fathers. This group included more than 50 (not 80) apocryphal gospels, with the Gospel of Thomas specifically singled out by Eusebius as part of this group.

The most ancient catalog of canonical works is the Muratorian Canon (c. AD 200). This record was discovered by Ludovico Muratori in the Ambrosian Library in Milan, and published by him in 1740. Though the first portion of the fragment is missing, it mentions Luke and John specifically as the third and fourth Gospels—strongly implying Matthew and Mark came before it. In fact, Irenaeus quotes directly from all four canonical Gospels 30 years *before* the Muratorian list.

The inclusion of John is ironic in light of Teabing's claims. The fourth Gospel is an irritation to liberal critics because of its "high Christology." It is replete with mentions of Jesus as the Son of God, an idea Teabing says didn't surface for centuries after John wrote.

If Brown is correct about the Nicaean conspiracy, we would not expect to see the four canonical Gospels singled out and affirmed early in the historical record. Yet that is exactly what we find.

Works like the Gospel of Phillip or the Gospel of Mary (Magdalene)—which feature so prominently in Brown's novel— were never taken seriously by the early church. Rather, they were opposed for a very good reason. They, like the other

Pseudepigrapha, were late-comers. They lacked any connection with the original apostles and contradicted the records written by those who were eyewitnesses to Jesus' life.

Why should we trust the Gospel of Phillip, for example, against Matthew, Mark, Luke, or John? Do we have evidence Philip and Mary are early, authentic, and reliable? How do we know they are unaltered, as Teabing assumes? Brown cannot just *say* these things; he must *show* these things. Unless, of course, he's simply writing a work of complete fiction.

No, the actual historical evidence shows an early consensus on the Gospels. The canonical Gospels had broad acceptance and were in early use by the church. The Gnostic Gospels like Thomas, Mary, and Philip were not. Nor were the "more than eighty gospels considered for the New Testament." Which is why, in actual fact, they were never considered at all.

Dating the Gospels

What of the historical accuracy of the canonical accounts of Jesus' life? The reliability of the details depends in part on another argument showing the gospels were written early, boosting their credibility over second century competitors like the Gospels of Philip and Mary.

This argument hinges on two facts virtually uncontested by anyone in academic circles. One, the Gospel of Luke and the book of Acts were written by the same author.[5] Simply compare the opening verses of Luke with the opening verses of Acts and you'll see the internal evidence. Two, the Apostle Paul was executed sometime during the Neronian persecution of the mid 60s. This also is not in dispute.

Here's the argument. First, the account in Acts ends abruptly with Paul in jail during his first Roman imprisonment. Why does the narrative just stop? Most likely because Luke had nothing more he could write since Acts 28 was "today" for him at the time he completed his history. This gives us an outside date for the completion of Acts at somewhere around 62 A.D.

Second, Luke's Gospel was written before Acts, placing it in the early 60s to late 50s. Third, even the most liberal critics place Mark and Matthew before Luke, with Mark generally considered the most ancient account.

This places the first gospels in the mid to late 50s and possibly much earlier, putting them, *on the outside*, only 30 years from the crucifixion—powerful evidence for their reliability. The shorter the time, the less likely the distortion, the less chance for accretion of legend and fanciful stories, especially with so many firsthand witnesses still alive, including most of the apostolic band.

Eminent New Testament scholar John A. T. Robinson gives another reason to be confident the Gospels were written early:

> *One of the oddest facts about the New Testament is that what on any showing would appear to be the single most datable and climactic event of the period—the fall of Jerusalem in A.D. 70, and with it the collapse of institutional Judaism based on the temple—is never once mentioned as past fact.*[6]

Since Luke recorded Jesus' prophesy of the temple's destruction (Luke 21:6), it is unthinkable he would not have pointed to its fulfillment had Jerusalem already fallen. Is it reasonable to believe not one Gospel writer would mention this to vindicate his message if the Gospels were late and this event had already taken place?

In fact, Robinson argues forcibly that every book of the New Testament was completed before 70. By contrast, no one places the Gnostic contenders earlier than the second century.

Teabing is wrong when he says, "There is no definitive account of the life of Jesus." We have four of them, written early, being actively used by the church centuries before Constantine.

The Bible's "Evolution"

In *The Da Vinci Code*, Sir Leigh Teabing states the Bible "has evolved through countless translations, additions, and revisions. History has never had a definitive version of the book." Is he right?

This charge has already been thoroughly answered elsewhere,[7] but here is a summary. We have thousands of Greek manuscripts of the New Testament, thousands of early translations, and thousands of citations by the early church fathers. If the Gospels were radically transformed, as Teabing says, we would expect to find radical discrepancies between the manuscripts that have survived. But we do not. The early minuscules (small Greek letters in cursive style) are virtually the same as the later uncial codices (manuscripts in capital Greek letters bound together in book form).

Dan Brown has not done his homework. He is simply mistaken in his assessment of the reliability of the New Testament documents. The biblical records actually show more textual integrity than any other work of antiquity that historians like Sir Leigh Teabing must rely on to ply their trade.

No evidence suggests the New Testament evolved over time through countless translations and revisions. Instead, the academic analysis shows it to be the most reliable document from antiquity. The Bible has not been changed.[8]

Playing Sherlock

You don't need to be a scholar to beat Dan Brown at his game. Do your own historical sleuthing. The primary source material is available to virtually anyone, especially if you have access to the internet. Nothing is hidden or suppressed. Many of the ancient documents are available in book form on Amazon.com or can simply be Googled.

In the *Anti-Nicene Fathers* you'll find ten full volumes of primary source documentation from before the Council of Nicaea (available in hardbound or on the internet) affirming the early belief that Jesus was the Son of God. These include *Against Heresies*, the vigorous refutation of Gnosticism by Irenaeus of Lyon (ca. 125-202), and *Against Praxeas* (c. 208), a polemic by Tertullian against modalism and for the Trinity.

The definitive source for early church history is Philip Schaff's *History of the Christian Church*. In Volume II, 548-556, Schaff chronicles the development of the doctrine of the divinity of Christ through the first three centuries before the Council of Nicaea. Find a detailed account of the Council proceedings themselves—drawn principally from the eyewitness accounts of two of the central players, Eusebius and Athanasius—in Volume III, 622-633.

Athanasius wrote two works on the deity of Christ—*Defense of the Nicene Definition* and *On the Incarnation of the Word*—powerful evidence the Nicene decision was theological, not political.

The original Dead Sea Scrolls can be found in the Rockefeller Museum and the Shrine of the Book, both in Jerusalem under the care of Israel, not the Vatican. Microfilm copies of the Scrolls are available in over 80 libraries around the world, including the Huntington Library in San Marino, California. Websites devoted to the Dead Sea Scrolls include the Israel Museum site, the Library of Congress site, and The Orion Center for the Study of the Dead Sea Scrolls.

For Gnostic texts use the Nag Hammadi Library Index Search at webcom.com/gnosis/naghamm/nhsearch.html.

For an exhaustive list (over 150 documents) of other early writings, some in their original languages with translation and commentaries including the Gospel of Phillip and the Gospel of Mary (Magdalene), go to earlychristianwritings.com.

It ought to be clear by now that Dan Brown, though a clever author, is no historian. Virtually nothing in *The Da Vinci Code* that touches Christianity or the Bible is sound. Indeed, every time Sir Teabing says dismissively, "It's a matter of historical record," be prepared for a complete fabrication.

The simple lesson is this: Read critically. Reflect on the claims. Check the background information. Assess the argument. Find the truth.

Enjoy the book, if you care to read it. But never forget, *The Da Vinci Code* is a work of *fiction*, nothing more.

Endnotes

1. Philip Schaff, *History of the Christian Church*, Vol. II (Grand Rapids: Eerdmans, 1910), 66, 68.

2. Ibid., 622-633. Schaff drew from the accounts of Eusebius and Athanasius.

3. "Nicaea did not settle the canon, as one might expect, but the Scriptures were regarded *without controversy* as the sure and immovable foundation of the orthodox faith." [emphasis added], Schaff, Vol. II, 523.

4. See Norman Geisler and William Nix, *A General Introduction to the Bible* (Chicago: Moody Press, 1986), ch. 17, and Schaff, Vol. II., 516-524, for a thorough discussion.

5. It is irrelevant to my point whether or not the author actually was Luke the "beloved physician" and companion of Paul, as the early church believed. The important thing is that Luke/Acts form a literary unit.

6. John A. T. Robinson, *Redating the New Testament* (Philadelphia: Westminster Press, 1976), 13.

7. See chapter titled "Can We Trust the New Testament Documents?"

8. For powerful arguments defending the integrity of the transmission along with a fascinating discussion on the question of canon, see Kostenberger and Kruger, *The Heresy of Orthodoxy* (Wheaton, IL: Crossway, 2010).

# No "Lost" Books

Are there lost books of the Bible? Has archaeology unearthed ancient texts that cast doubt on the current canon of Scripture? Is it possible that Christians don't have the true Word of God?

Many think so. History is written by the victors, they say. Early in the development of Christianity the "orthodox" group won the theological struggle, banned contrary ideas, purged dissent from their ranks, and burned "heretical" works. Some of the suppressed books survived, fortunately, allowing us to restore the so-called "lost books" of the Bible.

As it turns out, this is not a difficult challenge to parry. This particular assault on the canon can be answered by a close look at one word.

Browsing through the religious section in your local bookstore, you're likely to stumble on a handful of titles that suggest the discovery of "lost books" of the Bible. These recent works refer to ancient works that were "politically incorrect" according to the theological notions of the time. Branded as spurious by early church leaders, they were discredited and destroyed.

Luckily, these authors argue, a handful of copies survived. Rescued by archaeologists, the previously "lost books" of the Bible can now be restored to their rightful place in the canon. The *Gospel of Thomas*, unearthed in the Nag Hammadi library in Upper Egypt in 1945, would be a well-known example of one such lost-and-found ancient manuscript.

The suggestion that lost books of Scripture exist raises questions. It excites some people, but it jars others, sending a jolt through the system of the conscientious Christian. Could it be that archaeology has unearthed ancient biblical texts that cast doubt on the current canon of Scripture? Is it possible that the Bible Christians have come to count on is incomplete?

It might be hard to believe, but these questions can be answered without ever reading any of the "lost books" books in question. No research needs to be done, no ancient tomes addressed, no works of antiquity perused. Curiously, the entire issue can be answered by a close look at one word: Bible.

The Bible Divine

The whole question of alleged lost books of the Bible hinges on what one means by the word "Bible." It can only mean one of two things, it seems to me. There is a religious understanding of the word, and there is a more secular definition.

Ask an Evangelical Christian what the Bible is and he's likely to say simply, "It's God's Word." When pressed for a more theologically precise definition, he might add that God superintended the writing of Scripture so that the human authors, using their own style, personalities, and resources, wrote down, word for word, exactly what God intended them to write in the originals. This *verbal plenary inspiration* is a vital part of the classical Christian definition of the word "Bible."

For our purposes, the key notion in this definition is the phrase "exactly what God intended them to write." This is a critical element of this understanding of "Bible"—God was not limited by the fact that human authors were involved in the process.

Man's Mistakes

A common objection to the notion of inspiration is that the Bible was only written by men, and men make mistakes. This complaint misses the mark for two reasons.

First, it does not logically follow that because humans were involved in the writing process, the Bible must necessarily be in error. Mistakes may be *possible*, but they're not *necessary*. To assume error in all human writing is also self-defeating. The humanly derived statement, "The Bible was written by men, and men make mistakes," would be suspect by the same standards. The fact is, human beings can and do produce writing with no factual errors. It happens all the time.

Second, the challenge that men make mistakes ignores the main issue—whether or not the Bible was written *only* by men. The Christian accepts that fallible humans authored the text, but denies that man's limitations are significant in this case because inspiration guarantees that God's power supersedes man's liabilities.

A simple question—Columbo style—serves to illustrate this point: "Are you saying that if God exists, He's not capable of writing what He wants through imperfect men?"

This seems hard to affirm. The notion of an omnipotent God not being *able* to accomplish such a simple task is ludicrous. If, on the other hand, the answer is "No, I think He is able," then the objection vanishes. If God is capable, then limits on man are not a limit on God.

The divine inspiration of the Bible—if we can offer good reasons the Bible was from God to begin with—automatically solves the problem of human involvement. If God ensures the results, it doesn't matter if men or monkeys do the writing, they will still write exactly what God intends. That is part of what it means for the Bible to be divinely inspired.

The important thing for our purpose here is not to defend the notion of divine inspiration, but to understand that God's authorship and supernatural preservation are *entailed* in the first definition of the word "Bible." The Bible is the 66 individual books contained under one cover that are inspired by God, and are preserved and protected by His power. On this understanding, man's limitations are irrelevant.

Note again, I am not arguing for inspiration or even assuming it. I am simply clarifying one meaning of the word "Bible."

🏃 The Bible Secular

The second definition of the word "Bible" is not religious, and therefore includes no supernatural explanation for the Scripture. This view says that while Christians treated the Scriptures as divinely inspired, they were mistaken. The Bible merely represents a human consensus, a collection of books chosen by the early church to reflect its own beliefs (the history-is-written-by-the-victors approach).

A book that didn't make the cut was rejected ultimately for one basic reason: Early Christians didn't accept its theology. The motivation was human and political, not divine and supernatural. Christianity is no different from other religions that have collections of authoritative writings. Even individual professions identify certain books—bibles, if you will—as official representations of their respective fields. The Bible, then, is in that category—merely a collection of books chosen by the early church leaders to represent their own beliefs.

So we have two possible meanings for the word "Bible," a supernatural one and a natural one. Either the word "Bible" means something that is divinely given and divinely preserved— the conservative Christian view—or it refers to a collection of merely human documents representing the beliefs of a religious group known by the label "Christian"—the view of just about everyone else. Given either of these two definitions, could any books of the Bible be *lost*?

No Lost Books

Start with the first meaning, the supernatural definition of the Bible. Is it possible that books could be lost from a Bible of this sort? The answer is certainly no. Remember, on this view God Himself is supernaturally preserving and protecting the integrity of His work.

Regardless of whether the Christian claim about inspiration is accurate or not, it is obvious that on this definition it is not possible God would misplace His own book. The "lost books" thesis would thus be reduced to, "Certain books almighty God was responsible to preserve and protect got lost."

This is silly. The view makes God both almighty and inept at the same time. If the Bible is in fact the inspired Word of God, then the power of God Himself guarantees that no portion of it will ever be lost. There will always be a fully adequate testimony of His Word in every generation.

Could there be lost books given the second definition? What if Christians are wrong in attributing God's stewardship to the Scriptures? What if the Bible ultimately turns out to be merely a product of human design? If that's the case, then the term "Bible" refers not to the Word of God (the first definition), but to the canon of beliefs of the winners of the theological war, the leaders of the early church (the second definition). Is it possible that books could be lost from a Bible of this sort?

The answer again is certainly not. The "lost books" thesis would be reduced to this: "Early church leaders rejected certain books as unrepresentative of their beliefs that they actually believed reflected their beliefs"—another contradiction.

If the Bible is a collection of books the early church leaders decided would represent their point of view, then they have the final word on what is included. Any books they rejected were never part of *their* Bible to begin with, so even by the second definition, "lost books of the Bible" would be a misnomer.

Consider this scenario. You decide to write a book about your personal beliefs drawing from stacks of notes containing scattered reflections you've collected over the years. After editing and expanding on the ideas you finally settle on, you discard the rest. Later, someone rummaging through your trash comes upon your discarded notes. Could he claim he'd stumbled upon your lost beliefs?

"No," you'd respond, "these were not lost. They were rejected. If they were really my beliefs, they'd be in the book, not in the garbage."

Ironically, "lost books" advocates often point out that rediscovered texts were missing because the early church fathers suppressed them. It's true; they did. Critics think this strengthens their case, but it doesn't. Instead, it weakens their position by demonstrating that the "lost books" were not lost, but discarded, rejected as contrary to accepted Christian standards.

The early church acted fully within its authority when it rejected as non-canonical the Gospel of Thomas, for example, and other similar books. The leaders rightfully decided these writings did not represent their views. Therefore, they did not belong in the Christian Bible. And if they never were *in* the Bible in the first place, they couldn't be lost *from* the Bible.

🐾 Recall Vote?

Another approach to Scripture is worth mentioning. Some academics, like those of the Jesus Seminar, reject the idea that the Bible has supernatural origins. Since the Bible is just man's opinion anyway, why not have a recall vote? Amend the text to fix what is now considered defective or out of step with the times.

Such a reshuffling of the biblical deck—tossing out some books and including others to reflect what the church currently believes about spiritual truth—is certainly an alternative on a naturalistic view of the Scripture. If the members of the Jesus Seminar want to include the Gospel of Thomas in *their* bible, they're welcome to. Keep in mind though, they would not be restoring a "lost book" of the Bible, but merely redefining the canon to fit modern tastes.

✦ Lost and Found?

Regardless of how you view the Scripture—as supernatural or as natural—there is no sense in which there could be lost books of the Bible. If the Bible is supernatural—if God is responsible for its writing, its transmission, and its survival—then God, being God, doesn't fail. He doesn't make mistakes. He doesn't forget things. And He's not constrained by man's limitations. God can't lose His lessons.

However, if the Bible is not supernatural—as many will contend, especially those who claim to have found lost books—one faces a different problem. By what standard do we claim these are bona fide lost books of the canon of the early church? If, from a human perspective, the Bible is that collection of writings reflecting the beliefs of early Christianity, then any writings discarded by the church fathers are not books of their Bible by very definition.

Has archaeology unearthed previously unknown ancient texts? Certainly. Are they interesting, noteworthy, and valuable? Without question. Are they missing books of the Bible? The answer to that question is no. Two thousand years later, the rediscovery of something like the Gospel of Thomas may be archaeologically significant. It might be a lost book of antiquity, a great find, even a wonderful piece of literature.

But it is not a lost book of the Bible.[1]

Endnotes

1. Again, to be clear, I have not made the case for the ultimate authority of the canonical works. I have merely argued that the notion of lost books of the Bible is a contradiction, whether one thinks the Bible has a supernatural origin or not.

Archaeology, the Bible, and the Leap of Faith

Does the archeological accuracy of the Bible have anything to do with its truth claims? Not according to many world-class archaeologists. There's a catch, however, which tells us volumes about modern man and his dilemma.

I have held for a long time—along with many Christian apologists—that archaeology is a great ally of Christians. It bolsters the authority of the Bible because it consistently vindicates the historical accuracy of Scripture.

Imagine my shock when I learned that many world-class archaeologists disagree.

I was flying to Israel reading an article in the 20th anniversary issue of *Biblical Archaeology Review* [1] in which scholars addressed three issues: the greatest achievements of biblical archaeology, its greatest failures, and the challenges it continues to face. As I read through the article, I noticed two themes unfold.

The first was a concern voiced by many of the contributors— some of them Jewish archaeologists, some Christian (though not Evangelical or conservative)—who bemoaned the attempts of "fundamentalists" to use archaeology to "prove" the religious claims of the Bible.

This was an embarrassing revelation to me because I had been advocating that very thing. Yet here were prominent archaeologists saying this misuse of their discipline deeply annoyed them.

There was a catch, though—the second theme. These same archaeologists continued to maintain with equal conviction that their research had confirmed, by and large, that the history of the Bible was sound.

✦ Confused Convictions

Sometimes these two themes were played out side by side. Menahem Mansoor, a professor emeritus at the University of Wisconsin at Madison, said:

> Biblical archaeology's greatest significance is that it has corroborated many historical records in the Bible. Biblical archaeology has failed to deter people who seek to validate religious concepts by archaeological finds. These people should not confuse fact with faith, history with tradition, or science with religion.[2]

Israel Finkelstein, co-director of excavations at Tel Megiddo and professor of archaeology at Tel Aviv University, said:

> The most obvious failure [of archaeology] has been the abuse of the "old Biblical archaeology" by semi-amateur archaeologists. I refer to the romantic days when a special breed of archaeologists roamed the Middle East with a spade in one hand and the Scriptures in the other. These were the times of desperate attempts to prove that the Bible was correct.[3]

David Ussishkin, professor of archaeology at Tel Aviv University, made similar comments about the problems of drawing religious conclusions based on the historical evidence in the Scriptures, yet at the same time made this interesting admission:

> A fundamental question asked all over the world during the last two centuries is, Is the Bible true? Do the narratives related in it represent real events and are the figures mentioned there real people who lived and acted as the Biblical text tells us they did?... In general, the evidence of material culture fits the Biblical account beginning with the period of the settlement of the tribes of Israel in the land of Canaan and the establishment of the kingdom of Israel. Hence, archaeological data are consistent with the view that at least this part of the Biblical account is, in general, true and historically based.[4]

Aren't these statements odd? These eminent scholars admit archaeological evidence demonstrates that the historical record of the Bible is reliable, by and large. Yet they add a disclaimer warning us not to draw religious conclusions from the accurate history in the Scriptures.

My question is, "Why not?" Because, they say, this would be confusing history with religion, facts with faith.

Yet isn't this precisely the point of the biblical narrative? Isn't this the unique feature of Judaism (and, by extension, Christianity), that its religious claims are rooted in history? Isn't this the dramatic difference between the distant God of the deist and the living, active, personal Protector of Israel? The God of the Hebrews is not like the gods of wood and stone. Yahweh acts, leaving His fingerprints on history in ways that can be measured and quantified.[5]

🏃 Seeing the Unseen

We learn a lesson regarding this from Jesus. In the Gospel of Mark, Jesus caused a stir when He forgave the sins of a paralytic. As the scribes noted, forgiving sins was God's privilege, not man's. Further, how could anyone know if Jesus was telling the truth? It's easy to make claims about an invisible realm that can't be tested.

Jesus understood this, so He gave the people some tangible evidence. He said, "'In order that you may know that the Son of Man has authority on earth to forgive sins'—He said to the paralytic—'I say to you, rise, take up your pallet and go home'" (Mk. 2:10-11).

This supernatural healing was an historical event, what Jesus' biographers called an "attesting miracle." Jesus gave them something they could see in the physical realm to substantiate a claim He was making about something they couldn't see in the spiritual realm. History proved religion. Facts substantiated faith.

The historical record in the Hebrew Bible (the Old Testament) serves the same purpose. The great redemptive act in the history of the Jews was their escape from slavery in Egypt. In the writings of Moses we find an historical record of the events leading up to this exodus.

If we could show that these events took place largely as described in this account—that ten plagues culminating in the death of the firstborn of pharaoh shook the foundation of the greatest nation on earth at the time, and that the Hebrews then escaped across the sea with the Egyptian army destroyed in its wake—wouldn't it be fair to say this history has "religious" significance?

The record itself claims as much. In Exodus 9:14 we find this statement: "For this time I will send all My plagues on you and your servants and your people, *so that you may know* that there is no one like Me in all the earth." Once again, a series of observable, historical events (plagues) were meant to verify unobservable, spiritual truths.

The resurrection of Jesus of Nazareth works the same way in the New Testament. If, using the accepted canons of historical research, we demonstrate that Jesus rose from the dead—as four different, carefully detailed records of Jesus' life claim—wouldn't it be reasonable to conclude that this fact has something to do with the veracity of the Christian faith?

The apostle Paul thought so. He said that if Jesus had not risen from the dead, then Christians, of all people, ought to be pitied.[6] The truthfulness of Christianity—just like the truthfulness of ancient Judaism—is necessarily tied to historical events. These redemptive claims cannot be separated from the facts of history, because history is a record of the redemptive acts themselves.

Strange Schizophrenia

When world-class archaeologists acknowledge that their research largely supports the Bible's historicity, and then in the next breath warn, "This doesn't mean the Bible is true," they admit to a strange schizophrenia.

Dr. Francis Schaeffer described this malady in a little book titled *Escape from Reason*. Schaeffer's analysis helps us understand why, on the one hand, archaeologists say the Bible is accurate—that their craft has overwhelmingly demonstrated the reliability of the Bible as an historical text—yet, on the other hand, continue to assert this has nothing to do with the truthfulness of Scripture in spiritual matters.

Schaeffer explains that modern man lives in an oddly fractured world. His life is lived on two different planes. Picture a two-story house with no staircase connecting the upper story with the lower story. The lower story consists of one kind of reality—facts, science, the laws of nature, rationality, logic, the world as it really is. The upper story is where values, meaning, religion, faith, morality, and God reside.

The tragedy of modern thinking is that there is no way to bring the two together. Schaeffer calls this the "line of despair." There is no way to extract transcendent meaning from the mere facts of life. There is no way to infer religion or morality from the details of the world as it really is. The line that separates the lower story from the upper story is absolute and impermeable.

Modern man is split in two. In the lower story—the "real" world—he is imprisoned in a machine-like universe of cause and effect, matter in motion. His life is determined by natural forces which cannot be violated and which he cannot control. Mankind is dust in the wind, leading to despair.

Modern man's only hope is what Schaeffer calls the "upper-story leap." Meaning and significance cannot be found in the facts of the real world. Therefore, they must be fabricated by our imagination and believed against all fact and reason. Man invents significance, value, and morality for himself by making an irrational, blind leap of faith into the upper story. This alone gives hope, but it's only a placebo. It gives nothing substantial to answer our despair. It only makes us feel better for the moment, as long as we don't think too hard about the true consequences of our leap.

Listen to Schaeffer's sober description of the plight of modern man:

> *What we are left with runs something like this: Below the line there is rationality and logic. The upper story becomes the nonlogical and the nonrational. There is no relationship between them. In other words, in the lower story, on the basis of all reason, man as man is dead. You have simply mathematics, particulars, mechanics. Man has no meaning, no purpose, no significance. There is only pessimism concerning man as man. But up above, on the basis of a nonrational, nonreasonable leap, there is a nonreasonable faith which gives optimism. This is modern man's total dichotomy.*[7]

🐾 Faith in the Real World

This theme plays itself out daily in our culture. Pick up any newspaper or tune in to any talk show where moral or religious issues are being discussed. You'll see this upper-story leap in evidence.

In the *Los Angeles Times* one writer, commenting on the Pope and Catholicism, gave the "fashionable" perspective: "Religions are concerned with spiritual matters that are subjective, personal, and private. One need have no proof or justification for one's spiritual beliefs, because no one has the right to presume to judge the validity of those beliefs."[8]

To this writer, religious claims are in a separate category from fact. Spiritual beliefs are inventions of one's own mind or blind leaps of faith. In neither case do they have any rational or reasonable connection with the real world. Therefore, there can be no objective foundation from which to make judgments.

The writer is unwittingly describing Schaeffer's upper story. Belief can't be analyzed by fact or by argument because ultimately there is no relationship between religious belief and fact. There is no connection between the content of the upper story—value, meaning, significance, morals, religion, God— and the facts of the real world in the lower story.   To suggest otherwise is foolish, false, and in today's culture, rude and intolerant (an unfortunate moral judgment that can have no basis in reality on their view, by the way).

Even our legal system operates by these rules. Gone is the confidence of our founders who wrote, "We hold these truths to be self-evident, that all men are created equal, that they are endowed by their Creator with certain unalienable rights." The men responsible for the Declaration of Independence held that the transcendent truths which were the foundation of the Revolution were also facts of the real world, facts so real they staked their lives, their fortunes, and their sacred honor on them. No line of despair here.

That has radically changed, though. In a recent Supreme Court case, the court ruled, "At the heart of liberty is the right to define one's own concept of existence, of meaning, of the universe, and of the mystery of human life."[9] Even the Supreme Court admitted that issues of the upper story are completely subjective. We've gone from self-evident, transcendent truths to every man defining truth for himself.

This same "upper-story leap" is echoed in modern science. The late Stephen Jay Gould—outspoken Harvard paleontologist and popular writer on evolution—claimed:

> *Before Darwin, we thought that a benevolent God had created us. [Now we know that] no intervening spirit watches lovingly over the affairs of nature, (though*

Newton's clock-winding God might have set up this machinery at the beginning of time and then let it run). No vital forces propel evolutionary change. And whatever we think of God, His existence is not manifest in the products of nature.[10]

In spite of statements like these, Gould held that evolution presents no threat to religion, and that many of his colleagues believe in God. How can we make sense out of Gould's apparently contradictory views? It only makes sense if "God beliefs" are not in the real world of the lower story, but in the "faith" world of the upper story.

Notice the impermeable barrier between the upper and lower stories. The world evolved by natural laws. Divine intentions had nothing to do with it. Believers are welcome to cling to the idea of God as long as they understand that their religious language has nothing to do with reality. It's just a religious placebo. In the real world we know better. We're the mindless product of molecules clashing in the universe. Nothing more.

The schizophrenia of modern man permeates the public discourse and influences the disciplines of science and the dictates of law. We shouldn't be surprised, then, to find the same thing in history and archaeology.

Restoring Harmony

The archaeologists I cited implicitly hold that religious truth has nothing to do with reality. The Bible is accurate where it touches history, but it is a misuse of archaeology, they claim, to suggest that such things can substantiate one's private, personal, upper-story leap of faith.

Why do these scholars hold this? Because they must. They are modern men.

There's a reason the Bible is a record of history and not merely a list of religious beliefs. God has tied religious claims—which can't easily be tested—to historical events—which can be verified to a significant degree.

By their very nature the events of the Bible have ramifications for transcendent truth. If Jesus rose from the dead as a point of historical fact, intellectual honesty requires we not dismiss it as an interesting but meaningless fact of history. Instead, we are forced to concede with the apostle Paul that Jesus of Nazareth was "declared the Son of God with power by the resurrection from the dead."[11]

For the Christian, there is no "second story leap." Instead, there is harmony between our spiritual convictions and the particulars of our world. Archaeology—along with recorded history, science, philosophy, etc.—gives our faith a real purchase point, a secure footing. We are not just guessing. We're not making this up. We're not merely emoting. The truths of history and the truths of Christianity are linked together, both part of the real world.

Endnotes

1. *Biblical Archaeology Review*, May/June 1995.

2. Ibid., 29.

3. Ibid., 27.

4. Ibid., 32.

5. I should note that there is controversy in academic circles about the accuracy of both the Gospels (by the "Jesus Seminar," etc.) and the Hebrew Scriptures (by the "minimalist" school). These critiques are deeply tainted by a naturalistic (anti-supernatural) bias and, especially in the case of the Old Testament, a refusal to accept any biblical account without independent corroboration, a virtual impossibility when dealing with texts this ancient. A more even-handed approach to the accounts using the standard criteria of historiography minus the naturalistic bias yields high marks for the Bible as an historical source.

6. 1 Corinthians 15:19.

7. Francis Schaeffer, Escape from Reason, in The Complete Works of Francis Schaeffer (Wheaton, IL: Crossway Books, 1968), vol. 1, 237-8.

8. *L.A. Times*, April 27, 1995.

9. *Casey vs. Planned Parenthood.*

10. Quoted in Phillip Johnson, *Reason in the Balance* (Downers Grove, IL: InterVarsity Press, 1995), 75.

11. Romans 1:4.

ever Read a Bible Verse

Evangelicals have developed a dangerous habit of looking for verses or isolated phrases in their Bibles that they think the Spirit "impresses" on them with personal messages foreign to the original context. Experiences like these are powerful, but problematic.

The Bible itself teaches that God chose specific words meant to communicate precise meanings. Looking for private messages in passages originally intended to mean something else interferes with that divine intent. Instead, the Bible tells us to study to get the correct sense of a passage. Then we are to guard and protect that truth from distortion and abuse.

One simple rule of thumb will keep you on the right track.

If there was one bit of wisdom, one rule of thumb, one single skill I could impart, one useful tip I could leave that would serve you well the rest of your life, what would it be? What is the single most important practical lesson I've ever learned as a Christian that I can pass on to you? Here it is: *Never read a Bible verse.* That's right, never read a Bible *verse.* Instead, always read a paragraph—at least—if you want to unlock the meaning of a passage.[1]

Think of it this way. When you stumble into the middle of a conversation and hear a phrase or a sentence that piques your curiosity, what question do you ask? You ask, "What are you talking about?" You instinctively know you need the context to make sense of the conversation and benefit from it.

The same is true when we stumble into the middle of a Bible passage. We can't know what the writer is talking about by looking at an isolated sentence or phrase. An individual verse is only one part of the flow of thought. We usually have to take the bigger picture into account to have any hope of understanding the message.

This works because of a basic rule of all communication: Meaning always flows from the top down, from the larger units to the smaller units, not the other way around. The key to the meaning of any verse comes from the paragraph, not just from the individual words.

✼ My Radio "Trick"

When I'm on the radio, I use this simple rule—"Never read a Bible verse"—to help me answer Bible questions I'm asked, even when I'm unfamiliar with the passage. I call it my radio "trick." It's an amazingly effective technique you can use, too.

Here it is: I turn to the passage in question and I read the whole paragraph, not just the single sentence or phrase. I take stock of the relevant material above and below the reference I'm asked about. Since the context frames the verse and gives it specific meaning, I let it tell me what's going on. Sometimes the most obscure passages come into focus with this simple technique.

The numbers in front of the sentences in your Bible give the illusion that the verses stand alone in their meaning. Verse numbers were not in the originals, though. They were added hundreds of years later. As a result, chapter and verse breaks sometimes pop up in unfortunate places, separating relevant material that should be grouped together.

In order to employ the simple rule, "Never read a Bible verse," ignore the verse numbers and try to get the big picture by looking at the larger unit. Then narrow your focus. It's not very hard or time consuming. It takes only a few minutes of careful reading. [2]

It works like this. Begin with the broad context of the book. What type of literature is it—history? poetry? proverb? Different genres require different approaches.

Next, stand back from the verse and look for breaks in the text that identify major units of thought, then focus on the section your verse is part of. Take in at least a paragraph, maybe more. In narrative passages (like the Gospels, Acts, or much of the Old Testament), you might need to survey the whole chapter.

Finally ask, *"What in this paragraph or group of paragraphs gives any clue to the meaning of the verse in question?"* Look especially at the flow of thought in the passage. What ideas are in play and how are they being developed?

There is a reason this little exercise is so important. Words have different meanings in different contexts (that's what makes puns work). When we consider a verse in isolation, one meaning may occur to us. But how do we know it's the right one? Help won't come from the dictionary. Dictionaries only complicate the issue, giving us more choices, not fewer. Help must come from somewhere else, but it's not very far away. It comes from the surrounding paragraphs.

✒ The Paraphrase Principle

With the larger context now in view, you can speculate on the meaning of the verse itself, then test your interpretation by employing what I call "the paraphrase principle." It's an incredibly simple way to find out if your take on the text is in the running.

Good interpretations are nothing more than accurate paraphrases. They say essentially the same thing the verse does, but in other words. So put that insight to work.

When you think you have a handle on the author's intent based on your analysis—your careful observation, research, and study—in context, sum up his meaning in your own words. Then, *replace the text in question with your paraphrase* and see if the passage still makes sense in light of the larger flow of thought. Is it intelligible when inserted back into the paragraph? Does it dovetail naturally with the bigger picture? If it doesn't, you know you're on the wrong track. This technique will immediately weed out interpretations that are obviously erroneous.[3]

Here is an example of how the paraphrase principle can effectively clear up a common misunderstanding.

✒ A "Spirit of Fear"

In 2 Timothy 1:7 we read, "For God has not given us the spirit of fear, but of power, and of love, and of a sound mind" (KJV). Some have taken Paul to mean that whenever a believer feels fearful, it is the result of a demonic "spirit of fear" that needs to be resisted, bound, or even cast out.

The word "spirit," though, has more than one meaning, so it's open to more than one interpretation. "Spirit" could mean an immaterial, spiritual person—a demonic spirit, an angel, the Holy Spirit, a human soul, etc. (e.g., Luke 4:33, Acts 16:16), which is the sense taken in the interpretation above. However, "spirit" could also mean a disposition, frame of mind, mood, or defining characteristic. In 1 Cor. 4:21, Paul talks about dealing with the errant Corinthians either "with a rod or with love and a spirit of gentleness"(see also Gal. 6:1, Rom. 8:15).

The important question is this: What sense of the word "spirit" does Paul have in mind when writing to Timothy? The paraphrase principle comes to our rescue.

Here's our paraphrase of the first option: "For God hath not given us *the demonic spirit of fear*, but *a demonic spirit [an angelic spirit?] of power, and of love, and of a sound mind.*" This seems odd. Does the Bible teach that the qualities of power, love, and a sound mind are the result of spiritual beings that influence or have power over us, or are they virtuous dispositions we develop and possess?

Let's try the alternate meaning: "For God hath not given us *a timid and fearful disposition,* but *a disposition of power, and of love, and of a sound mind.*" This makes perfect sense, especially when you consider the larger context (remember, "Never read a Bible verse"), which includes Paul's admonition that Timothy not be ashamed of the testimony of our Lord (v. 8).

Paul is talking about timidity, not spirits. Timothy was not being harassed by a demonic spirit called "fear." He was faint-hearted. This is why the NASB renders the verse, "For God has not given us a spirit of *timidity*, but of power and love and discipline."[4]

☂ Having a "Peace" about It

Colossians 3:15 is a text that is constantly misunderstood by well-meaning Christians. Paul writes there, "Let the peace of Christ rule in your hearts." Some have accurately pointed out that the Greek word for "rule" means to act as arbiter or judge. They see this verse as a tool for knowing God's will for our lives.

The conventional thinking goes something like this. An internal sense of peace acts like a judge helping us to make decisions according to God's will. When confronted with a decision, pray. If you feel peace in your heart, take it as a green light. God is giving you the go-ahead. If you don't feel peace, don't proceed.

This inner tranquility, then, acts like a judge helping you make decisions consistent with God's purposes. On this interpretation, a paraphrase might be: "And let feelings of peacefulness in your heart be the judge about God's individual will for your life." Is that what Paul has in mind?

This is a classic example of how a little knowledge of Greek can be dangerous if context is not taken into consideration. The Greek meaning of "rule" is not the relevant detail of this passage. Rather, the meaning of the word "peace" is the critical issue. It actually has two different meanings.

"Peace" could mean a sense of inner harmony and emotional equanimity. Paul seems to have this definition in mind in Philippians 4:7: "And the peace of God, which surpasses all comprehension, shall guard your hearts and your minds in Christ Jesus." This is the *subjective* (what you feel) sense of peace.

The word "peace" also has an *objective* sense: lack of conflict between two parties formerly in conflict with each other. This definition is what Paul intends in Romans 5:1: "Therefore having been justified by faith, we have peace with God through our Lord Jesus Christ." (Note the distinction between the peace *of* God and peace *with* God in these two verses.)

Here is our question: What sense of peace did Paul have in mind when writing this admonition to the Colossians? The Greek gives no indication because the same word (*eirene*) is used in each case. Once again, context solves the problem. The specific meaning can only be known by looking at the surrounding material.

What clues can we find in the larger context? Well, in verse 11, Paul says that in the Body of Christ there are no *divisions* between Greek and Jew, slave and free, etc. On this basis he appeals for *unity* in the church characterized by forgiveness, humility, and gentleness. He then adds that peace should be the ruling principle (the arbiter or judge) informing those relationships.

It seems clear that Paul has in mind the objective sense of "peace" here—lack of conflict between Christians—not a subjective feeling of peace in an individual Christian's heart. Let's find out. What do we discover when we join the suggested paraphrases with the context?

> Put on a heart of compassion, kindness, humility, gentleness, and patience; bearing with one another, and forgiving each other, whoever has a complaint against

anyone. Just as the Lord forgave you, so also should you. And beyond all these things put on love, which is the perfect bond of unity. And *let feelings of peacefulness in your heart be the judge about God's individual will for your life*, to which indeed you were called in one body. And be thankful.

vs.

Put on a heart of compassion, kindness, humility, gentleness, and patience, bearing with one another, and forgiving each other, whoever has a complaint against anyone. Just as the Lord forgave you, so also should you. And beyond all these things put on love, which is the perfect bond of unity. And *let harmony, not conflict, be the rule that guides you* [plural], to which indeed you were called in one body. And be thankful.

The first is completely foreign to the context; the second fits right in with everything that comes before and after. In the context of Colossians 3, there is no hint of using internal feelings as a divine stamp of approval on our decisions. Personal decision-making is not the message of the paragraph. Harmony and unity in the Body is.

Context Is King

Both of these examples illustrate a deeper truth about properly understanding the Bible, or any other communication for that matter: Context is king. The paraphrase principle works so well because it trades on the fact that the meaning of any particular word or phrase is always governed by the role it plays in the context of larger units like sentences and paragraphs.

Think of it this way: Wouldn't it be convenient to have a biblical "tour guide" on call to clear up confusion in the text any time you open your Bible, someone who could tell you the explicit meaning of a verse in many cases, or at least help you to know what the verse doesn't mean and thus narrow your options?

Wouldn't it be helpful to have a tutor who could point out critical clues to the meaning, identify conditions that constrain the application of the verse, or indicate the audience the verse may be limited to? If that sounds appealing, then pay attention to context, because it does each of these things. Let's look at them, one by one.

✒ "If I Be Lifted Up"

Context often clearly and unambiguously gives us the exact meaning of a phrase or passage. John 12:32 is a case where a phrase can have two widely divergent meanings, yet right in the text the author reveals precisely what he has in mind.[5]

"If I be lifted up…I will draw all men to Myself," is one of Jesus' statements that worship leaders often cite. They explain that in worship we "lift up" the Lord when we exalt Him and declare His glory. If we focus on Jesus and ascribe glory to Him, the power of Christ is released to transform the hearts of those listening and they are drawn to Him.

Now, there is no question in my mind that worship performs this function, which is why worship leaders assume this meaning. But is this the meaning *Jesus* had in mind? It's not. I know because I kept reading. John tells us in the very next verse precisely what Jesus meant: "But He was saying this to indicate *the kind of death* by which He was to die."

When we apply our paraphrase test, the results look like this: "'And I, *if I be exalted before the people*, will draw all men to Myself.' But He was saying this to indicate the kind of death by which He was to die."

Jesus wasn't executed by praise, but by a cross. In this instance, being "lifted up" clearly means to be crucified, not exalted.

Understanding this phrase in context sheds light on another familiar passage, John 3:14-15: "And as Moses lifted up [raised in the air] the serpent in the wilderness, even so must the Son of Man be lifted up [raised in the air] that whoever believes may in Him have eternal life." Our paraphrase looks like this: "And as Moses raised the serpent in the air in the wilderness, even so must the Son of Man be *raised in the air* [on a cross] that whoever believes may in Him have eternal life."

This makes perfect sense. Jesus had to be crucified before salvation could be offered, an appropriate lead-in to the next verse, John 3:16—the most famous salvation verse in the Bible.

There is something else I want you to see. If you had checked out John 12:32 on your own, you would have noticed that the worship leader did not quote the verse quite right. He left something out. The full text actually reads, "And I, if I be lifted up *from the earth*, will draw all men to Myself."

This passage is nearly always misquoted, albeit unwittingly. Inaccurate quoting, though, leads to inaccurate interpretations. Beware of ellipses—the three dots (…) that signal something has been left out of a quote—because the omission may be vital to a verse's meaning.

The Eliminator

Sometimes context eliminates possible options by clearly showing what a verse does *not* mean. In John 20:29, Jesus says to the no-longer-doubting Thomas, "Because you have seen Me, have you believed? Blessed are they who did not see, and yet believed."

These words are often taken as a criticism of those seeking evidence for faith. On this view, Jesus commended "blind" faith as more virtuous. But this interpretation is not possible in light of what John writes next:

> *Many other signs, therefore, Jesus also performed in the presence of the disciples which are not written in this book, but these [signs] have been written that you may believe that Jesus is the Christ, the Son of God, and that believing you may have life in His name.*

If Thomas wasn't to rely on evidence, then why did John say he included the evidence of miraculous signs expressly for the purpose of abetting belief?

No, Jesus was objecting to something else. Thomas's problem wasn't that he wanted evidence. Most likely his error was that he didn't believe the evidence already adequate to establish the fact of the resurrection: the testimony of his fellow disciples ("We have seen the Lord!" v. 25). Thomas demanded an extreme standard of proof: "Unless I shall see in His hands the imprint of the nails, and put my finger into the place of the nails, and put my hand into His side, I will not believe."

Whatever the meaning behind Jesus' words, it's clear He did not mean that a leap of faith is better than a reasoned response of trust. The context does not allow that interpretation.

Truth Shall Set You Free?

Contrary to popular belief, Jesus never taught that truth sets us free. His words in John 8:32, "You shall know the truth, and the truth shall make you free," are frequently read as a simple truism: Truth sets free. Learn the truth and freedom follows.

Context, our faithful guide, reveals a condition that limits the application of Jesus' remarks about the impact of truth. In this case, it's necessary to read above and below our passage to get the full force of Jesus' point:

> So Jesus was saying to those Jews who had believed Him, "If you abide in My word, then you are truly disciples of Mine, and you will know the truth, and the truth shall make you free." They answered Him, "We are Abraham's descendants and have never yet been enslaved to anyone. How is it that You say, 'You will become free'?" Jesus answered them, "Truly, truly, I say to you, everyone who commits sin is the slave of sin. The slave does not remain in the house forever. The son does remain forever. So if the Son makes you free, you will be free indeed. (John 8:31-36)

The context immediately reveals two things. First, the freedom Jesus speaks of is freedom from slavery to sin. Second, Jesus' promise is conditional: If we do one thing, then another thing follows. If the result is freedom from sin's slavery, what is the condition? In short, faithful discipleship. We are set free when we abide in (obey, live in accordance with) Jesus' word.

Many passages taken naively as unqualified promises actually have conditions attached to them. Claiming them out of context is a fruitless enterprise. If we haven't fulfilled the conditions, then the promise does not apply to us.

For Your Eyes Only

Sometimes reading the Bible accurately in context can have disheartening results. It's painful to discover that verses once cherished for the emotional comfort they give us turn out to have a completely different meaning altogether. This often happens with Old Testament promises or encouragements originally meant for others that we mistakenly claim as our own without qualification.

A prime example comes from the prophet Jeremiah, through whom God spoke these words: "'For I know the plans that I have for you,' declares the Lord, 'plans for welfare and not for calamity to give you a future and a hope'" (Jer. 29:11).

The key question here is who is the "you" that God had in mind when He spoke these wonderful words of consolation. A careful examination of the context gives us the answer. The promise was limited to the specific audience identified at the beginning of the chapter:

> *Now these are the words of the letter which Jeremiah the prophet sent from Jerusalem to* the rest of the elders of the exile, the priests, the prophets, and all the people whom Nebuchadnezzar had taken into exile from Jerusalem to Babylon....*Thus says the Lord of hosts, the God of Israel,* to all the exiles whom I have sent into exile from Jerusalem to Babylon...(Jer. 29:1, 4)

When we read the full section instead of just one Bible verse, the larger picture begins to unfold:

> *For thus says the Lord, "When seventy years have been completed for Babylon, I will visit you [the Jewish exiles] and fulfill My good word to you, to bring you [those who are being sent away] back to this place, for I know the plans that I have for you [the exiles being sent away]," declares the Lord "plans for welfare and not for calamity to give you a future and a hope. Then you [exiles] will call upon Me and come and pray to Me, and I will listen to you. And you will seek Me and find Me, when you search for Me with all your heart. And I will be found by you," declares the Lord, "and I will restore your fortunes and will gather you from all the nations and from all the places where I have driven you [Babylon, etc.]," declares the Lord, "and I will bring you back to the place [Jerusalem and Judea] from where I sent you into exile." (Jer. 29:10-14)*

Our faithful guide, context, tells us clearly what God had in mind. After 70 years of discipline, the Jewish exiles would be restored from Babylon to their homeland in Judea and prosper according to the plans—and prior promise—of the Lord.[6]

Jeremiah's promise was for the Jews in exile, not for storm-tossed Christians uncertain about their future. We may learn broader principles from passages like these, like the principle that God keeps His promises when He makes them—a valuable lesson for believers of all eras—but the particular promise in this passage is not for us.[7]

In times of distress or uncertainty, we would do better to focus on promises specifically directed to followers of Christ, verses like "Come to Me, all who are weary and heavy-laden, and I will give you rest" (Matt. 11:28), or "Lo, I am with you always, even to the end of the age" (Matt. 28:20).

The practice of citing a verse without addressing the role it plays in a passage is called "prooftexting." It's a dangerous habit. Simply "claiming" a verse doesn't make it our own.

Whether claiming promises during difficult times or citing verses to substantiate my own biblical views, I want to be confident the texts I use to prove my point actually mean what I think they mean. That's why I'm always on the alert when reading popular books written on biblical issues. Are the authors simply quoting verses to buttress their points (prooftexting), or are they interpreting their texts by carefully looking at the details of context in harmony with other relevant passages?

The Role of the Holy Spirit

Some think that the Holy Spirit is a substitute for careful Bible study, or that He uses the text to dispatch tailor-made private revelations for each believer. Neither of these is true.

It's not wise to ask the Spirit to simply give you the interpretation of a passage. He has not promised to do so. God will help us, but He won't do the work for us. This is why Paul tells Timothy, "Be *diligent* to present yourself approved to God as a *workman* who does not need to be ashamed, *handling accurately* the word of truth" (2 Tim. 2:15).

And it's not right to think the Holy Spirit will "repurpose" a passage to give you a private personal message unrelated to the original intent. Instead, the Spirit "illuminates"—sheds light on—the Word, helping us see what is *already there* in words the Holy Spirit Himself inspired through the initial writers (see 1 Cor. 2:10-16).

If you think God is telling you something through Scripture that is not connected to the meaning of the words in their context, it can't be God because He will not twist, distort, or redefine His own Word for your private consumption.

The Holy Spirit does not give new information not already resident in the inspired words. The curriculum, so to speak, is standardized for all Christians. Every person has equal access to the meaning. *There are no private messages in Scripture.* The applications may vary, but the meaning remains the same.

Remember our basic rule: "Never read a Bible verse." Always read the larger context and identify the flow of thought. Then you can focus on the individual verse.

If you will do this one thing—if you will read carefully in the context applying the paraphrase principle—you will begin to understand the Bible as God intended and Scripture will open up for you like never before. Without the bigger picture, though, you'll be lost.

Only when you are properly informed by God's Word the way it was written—in its context—can you be transformed by it. Every piece becomes powerful when it is working together with the whole as the Holy Spirit intended.

It's the most important practical spiritual lesson I've ever learned...and the single most important thing I could ever teach you.

Endnotes

1. Notice I didn't say "Never *quote* a Bible verse." Rather, beware of simply reading the verse expecting to get the accurate meaning in isolation from the rest of the passage.

2. For a thorough treatment, I recommend Klein, Blomberg, and Hubbard's *Introduction to Biblical Interpretation* (Nashville: Thomas Nelson, 1993).

3. There is one limitation with the paraphrase test. It is not a foolproof *positive* test for accuracy. Some faulty interpretations can still slip by and must be disqualified on other grounds. Rather, it is a reliable *negative* test. It will immediately eliminate alternatives that don't fit the flow of thought. All potential interpretations must pass the paraphrase test, but passing the test is no guarantee that a particular view is correct. It's only one of the tools in your tool box helping narrow down your options, but it's an important one.

4. The archaic rendering of the King James Bible creates unnecessary confusion for the modern reader. As one person put it, the KJV is a good choice for any reader who is 350 years old or older. All others would do better with a more recent version.

5. This happens with some frequency in Scripture. Compare Matt. 13:24-30 with 13:36-43 where Jesus gives an explicit interpretation of His own parable.

6. See the Abrahamic Covenant, Gen. 12:1-3, and 15:7-21.

7. To sharpen the point, the prophet Daniel confirms this meaning. He refers to the Jeremiah text in Daniel 9:1-2 and clearly understands it as applying to exiled Judah. He follows with his famous prayer of confession, repentance, and request for restoration of the exiles to the Promised Land.

# Silly Putty Bible Study

21st-Century kids have cell phones, DVD players, and Xboxes. When I was a kid we had simpler delights. One was a handful of malleable goo that could be pulled, twisted, or distorted into any shape imaginable. It was called Silly Putty.

Sadly, many Christians use their Bibles like Silly Putty. Just add the Spirit and the Bible becomes putty in their hands, able to be molded into almost anything at all. Rather than approaching Scripture as a treasure of truth for all Christians, some Evangelicals have the dangerous habit of searching the text for a personal "promise" or "word" of guidance from the Spirit that is unrelated to the text's original meaning.

Often, the results turn out to be silly. Other times, they are dangerous. Regardless of the outcome, this practice is always a bad habit.

Ironically, Evangelicals who pride themselves on being biblical literalists often feel comfortable fleeing the plain, literal sense of a passage whenever "the Spirit leads."

I'm talking about the habit of isolating verses or phrases from Scripture and, under the Spirit's influence (allegedly), finding in them personal messages unrelated to the original circumstances of the text.

For example, at a meeting in Simi Valley, California, a woman told me someone in her fellowship claimed God "gave her" a verse while seeking guidance for an adulterous relationship she was involved in (I'm not making this up). The verse said, "Put on the new man," which she did.

At another church a young man understood "Grace be with you" in 1 Timothy 6:21 to be God's "leading" to date a worship leader who'd caught his eye. Her name was Grace.

When I relate these two stories to audiences, I get two different responses.

The combined laughter and groaning in the first case is

appropriate. The abuse of the Bible in this case is so extreme it's simultaneously funny and tragic. In the second case I get chuckles, but it's clear to me some are not convinced anything is amiss. These cases do not seem parallel.

While the woman's attempt to validate a sinful relationship is obviously misguided, there is nothing morally questionable about the young man's designs on Grace. Maybe God *was* speaking to him through his verse. Who was I to say otherwise?

The ambivalence here is telling. The objection in the first case was to the *application* of the method (justifying adultery and divorce), but not to the *method* itself. The method was the same in both cases, and therein lies the problem.

According to this "Spirit-led" approach, the meaning of a passage, at least in some circumstances, is not based on a careful analysis of the passage in its context. Context is irrelevant according to this method.

On this view, the important thing is not learning what the Spirit was originally saying in the inspired *writings*. Rather, the key is determining what the Holy Spirit is allegedly "speaking" in the unique personal circumstances of particular *readers*.

Christians use this method all the time, as do pastors from the pulpit, even though they should know better (they never learned this in seminary). When the "Spirit begins to move," all standards used to discover the objective truth of God's Word go out the window and the subjective reigns.

When verses can have different meanings for different people based on Holy Spirit "promptings," it begins to undermine the truth of the "faith, which was once for all delivered to the saints" (Jude 3). There are as many "truths" as there are readers.

If I'm right on this, lots of quiet-time theologizing—not to mention a host of devotional writings—is seriously misguided. For many Christians, their moments of "truth" turn out to be moments of emotion-filled biblical fiction.

🐾 The Holy Spirit Giveaway

Here's how it works. Instead of studying to find the objective meaning of a passage and then making personal application of that scriptural truth to their lives, many Christians read the Bible looking for verses or isolated phrases that the Spirit allegedly "impresses" on them, conveying to them personal messages that are foreign to the context.

For example, a Christian woman who has been praying for her family's conversion stumbles upon Acts 16 during her quiet time. Her eyes settle on Paul's response to the Philippian jailer who asked, "What must I do to be saved?" "Believe in the Lord Jesus and you shall be saved," Paul answered, then added "you and your household" (v. 29-31).

Moved by these words, the woman begins to claim the "promise" that *her own* household will be saved, with the justification that "The Holy Spirit gave me this verse."

Why would she use that particular wording ("gave me") to describe what she experienced? Because in the normal, natural understanding of that passage, the verse wasn't hers to begin with.[1] Rather, she believes that, under the Spirit's influence, there was a mystical transformation that took place causing the meanings of the words to change just for her, conveying a private message not intended *by* the original author (Luke, in this case) and not intended *for* anyone else. It was a private message from God to her *incorporating* the words of the biblical text, but not previously *in* those words.

Notice, her confidence is not based on the objective meaning of the passage, but on the unique subjective meaning given to her by the Spirit, allegedly, in the moment. I—or any other Christian, for that matter—could not claim that verse for myself unless the Holy Spirit "gave" the verse to me in that way, as well.

Experiences like these are powerful because they seem intensely personal. But there's a problem: Acts 16:31 is not her promise. It's the Philippian jailer's promise, if a promise at all.[2] Using the passage as she has done is an abuse of God's Word. It's also deeply relativistic.

Relativism is the defining characteristic of the age, and has influenced the church in subtle yet profound ways. When an objective claim (a verse) communicates completely different meanings ("truths") to different subjects (people), that's relativism. Since truth is not in the objective meaning of the words, but in the personal, subjective experience of the reader— in this case, an experience allegedly caused by the Holy Spirit—a personal prompting can be "true for me, but not for you." Since there are different experiences for different people, there are different "truths" for each.

Let me speak plainly: *There is no biblical justification for finding private, personal messages in texts originally intended by God to mean something else.* This approach is the wrong way to read the Bible. One reason I know this is because of what the Bible teaches about itself.

The Bible on Bible Study

First, the Bible teaches that the written words of Scripture are inspired.

"All scripture [*graphe,* Gr.—the "writing"] is inspired by God" (2 Timothy 3:16). The wording here is important. Paul says that the *writing itself* is "God breathed," not the thoughts, impressions, or private messages that occur to us when we read the writing.

God told Moses to speak to Pharaoh the specific *words* of God: "I will be with your mouth, and teach you what you are to *say*" (Exodus 4:12). "Let them hear my *words*," God said later at Horeb, "so they may learn to fear me all the days they live on the earth" (Deuteronomy 4:10). These are the "living *words*" that Stephen claimed had been passed on to us (Acts 7:38).

God told Jeremiah, "Write in a book all the *words* I have spoken to you" (Jeremiah 30:2). He said to Isaiah, "My *words* which I have put in your mouth, shall not depart from your mouth, nor from the mouth of your offspring, nor from the mouth of your offspring's offspring" (Isaiah 59:21).

God has always been concerned with the words, because precise words are necessary to convey precise meaning. That's why Paul confidently refers to God's revelation not as words of human wisdom, but as "*words*...taught by the Spirit" (1 Corinthians 2:13).

Second, the Bible teaches it is important to accurately understand these inspired words of Scripture. Note Jesus in Luke 10:25-28:

And behold, a certain lawyer stood up and put Him to the test, saying, "Teacher, what shall I do to inherit eternal

*life?" And He said to him, "What is written in the Law?
How does it read to you?" And he answered and said,
"You shall love the Lord your God with all your heart,
and with all your soul, and with all your strength, and
with all your mind, and your neighbor as yourself." And
He said to him, "You have answered correctly."*

Jesus did not ask, "What does the Spirit say to you on this
issue?" He asked, "What is *written*? How does it *read*?" Then
He waited to see if the lawyer got it right.

There is a correct and incorrect way to read the Bible. Paul
tells Timothy to handle the Word accurately to avoid bringing
shame on himself (2 Timothy 2:15). Jesus scolded the Pharisees
for not understanding the Scripture properly. He then made an
argument for the resurrection that hinged on the tense of a word:
"I *am* the God of Abraham, and the God of Isaac, and the God of
Jacob. He is not the God of the dead, but of the living" (Matthew
22:29-32).

*Third, the Bible teaches that private interpretations do not
yield the accurate meaning.* Peter is clear on this point. He
writes:

> *But know this first of all, that no prophecy of Scripture
> is a matter of one's own interpretation, for no prophecy
> was ever made by an act of human will, but men moved
> by the Holy Spirit spoke from God. (2 Peter 1:20-21)*

Because there is a divine author behind prophecy, the Apostle
argues, there is a particular truth—a determinate meaning—that
God intends to convey. Individual, personalized interpretations
that distort this meaning only bring danger (note the reference to
false prophets and false teachers in the next verse).

The same reasoning applies to all Scripture, not just to words
of prophets, because the same rationale applies—the same
divine author stands behind the entire Bible.[3] The meaning
God originally intended through the inspired writers is the same
meaning for anyone reading the verse today.

Simply put, "a text cannot mean what it never meant."[4]
Whenever God speaks, He has a particular truth in mind that
fanciful interpretations obscure. We are not free to extract our
own personalized revelations from Scripture. The Holy Spirit did
not mean one thing when Paul wrote to the church at Ephesus,

for example, and then something entirely different when we read it 2000 years later.

Fourth, the Bible teaches we are to be diligent in study to get the accurate meaning.

The "good hand of the Lord" was upon Ezra specifically because Ezra "had set his heart to *study* the law of the Lord" (Ezra 7:9-10). The New Testament Bereans were called noble precisely because they went back to the words of the text, "*examining the Scriptures daily to see whether these things were so*" (Acts 17:11).[5]

In Paul's last words before his death he admonished Timothy to "be *diligent* to present yourself approved to God as a workman who does not need to be ashamed, handling accurately the word of truth" (2 Timothy 2:15).

Paul warned of a time when the church "will not endure sound doctrine," but instead will turn to "myths" that "tickle" the ears (2 Timothy 4:3). Truth is the antidote, he said, preached faithfully and accurately. Success in this depends on diligent work, not on "hearing" from the Spirit.

Fifth, the Bible teaches we must guard the accurate meaning from being distorted, twisted, or maligned. This is clear from a number of passages. Jude writes (1:3):

> *Beloved, while I was making every effort to write you about our common salvation, I felt the necessity to write to you appealing that you contend earnestly for the faith which was once for all delivered to the saints.*

Paul assured the Corinthians that he was "not walking in craftiness or *adulterating* the word of God" (2 Corinthians 4:2). By contrast, Peter warned that the "untaught and unstable" *distort* Paul's words—"to their own destruction," he adds (2 Peter 3:16).

Anticipating his imminent martyrdom, Paul told Timothy, "Retain the *standard of sound words* which you have heard from me....*Guard...the treasure* which has been entrusted to you" (2 Timothy 1:13-14).

Do you realize you cannot distort something unless it has a specific, correct meaning that is able to be twisted? You cannot retain the standard of sound words unless the words are the standard for accuracy. You cannot contend for the same sound doctrine for everyone that protects us from myths— a "faith which was once for all delivered to the saints"— if each individual Christian can receive his own personal message from the text.

Finally, the Bible never teaches the subjective, individualized interpretation approach.

Where does Scripture advance the idea that the Holy Spirit changes the meanings of the words of the text for individual readers? Where does the Bible teach that private messages lurk between lines wanting only the Holy Spirit's touch to bring them to light? Where does God's Word suggest the relativistic, take-the-verse-out-of-context-for-my-own-private-use approach? It's not there.

If you think God is telling you something through Scripture that is not connected to the meaning of the words in their context, it can't be God because He chose to communicate *through* language, not around it. God will not twist, distort, or redefine His own Word for our private consumption.

"We cannot make [the Bible] mean anything that pleases us, and then give the Holy Spirit 'credit' for it," Fee and Stuart write. "The Holy Spirit cannot be called in to contradict Himself, and He is the one who inspired the original intent."[6]

The Bible speaks clearly on this question. The written words of Scripture are God-breathed, chosen specifically by the Holy Spirit for their precision. There is a correct way to read them and an incorrect way. Private interpretations do not yield accurate meanings. Instead, diligent study and careful examination of the text deliver to us unadulterated truth, a treasure we are to guard and protect from shameful distortion and abuse.

🐒 The OT in the NT

How is it, then, that Old Testament verses cited by New Testament writers sometimes seem so far removed from their original context? This is a fair question to which there are a variety of possible explanations, depending on the citation. Most hinge on our core principle: Meaning is always based on the author's intent.

First, since the principle author of Scripture is God, He may have intended more than what the Old Testament authors were aware of at the time and may clarify His original meaning in subsequent writings.

Second, God may have intended multiple meanings or multiple levels of meaning, or an immediate literal sense and an additional spiritual sense, or possibly a double fulfillment (e.g., prophecy and apocalyptic literature). The New Testament writers have insight into these meanings that we do not because they were writing under the inspiration of the Holy Spirit. They had a direct connection, in a sense, to the Author's intent.

There are other possibilities. Sometimes when a writer notes that the Scripture has been "fulfilled," he may mean that a type has been fulfilled—a divinely inspired pattern or symbol—and not specific verses themselves. God's history sometimes repeats itself (e.g., Jeremiah 31:15 vs. Matthew 2:17-18).

A later author may not be *finding* new meaning in a text, but *giving* new meaning to it. For us, then, the question is what did Matthew mean in his *use* of Hosea (for example), not what Hosea originally meant.

In no case, however, are New Testament authors relativizing the text for their own private use. Rather, they seem to be revealing formerly hidden *objective* meanings in the text that might have been implicit, but are now made explicit for application to the whole Christian community. This notion of community is critical since I have been arguing that God does not take verses out of context *as a means of conveying private messages to individual readers*.

🐾 Making It Practical

First, don't look for private messages in the Bible. They're not there. Do not "claim" verses that are not intended for you or your circumstances. When others say "God gave me this verse" (or "God gave me this verse for you"), check to see if the context is being abused. If you suspect so, raise a question: "I'm curious. How exactly did you get that meaning/promise/application from this verse?"

Always direct the discussion back to the meanings of the words, sentences, and paragraphs as understood in their original context. Like the Bereans, examine the text.

When someone says "You're putting God in a box," tell them, "It's never a mistake to try to use God's Word the way He intends." Ironically, it's often the challenger who is putting God in the box of private interpretation, subjectivism, superstition, and error.

Purchase a book to help you with your own biblical interpretation skills, then study it and begin to apply it immediately.

✰ No Power in Words

Christians err in thinking the words of Scripture are somehow vested with power. Just speak the words—"claim the verse"— and power is released to serve us. This is not a biblical view of language. God's Word is alive, true enough, but in a very specific sense (see Hebrews 4:12-13). His words do not have a life of their own. There is only power in God, in whose mind the words originate.

Therefore, the words are only alive as they serve God's original intent. They only have power when used as God purposed. There is no power when God's words are twisted, distorted, or adulterated for our private use. We cannot claim divine authority for a verse when we are using it in a way God did not desire. This is not Christianity. It is superstition.

Anyone teaching the Bible out of context, therefore, is not teaching the Bible at all, regardless of how much they "baptize" their inventions with Holy Spirit language. A reflection on a Bible passage in a morning quiet time, a devotional reading, or a Sunday sermon may be edifying, encouraging, and uplifting. But if it's not the message of the text—God's message—it lacks power even when it's quoted "chapter and verse."

There is a legitimate activity of the Holy Spirit making unique, personal *application* in our lives. But this is based on the *objective* meaning of a passage. The Spirit does not give new information not already resident in the inspired words. The curriculum, so to speak, is standardized for all Christians. Every person has equal access to the meaning, at least in principle. The Spirit "illuminates"—sheds light on—the Word, helping us to see what is already there in words the Spirit Himself inspired through the initial writers (see 1 Corinthians 2:10-16). He then aids us in personal application.

🐉 Wielding the Sword

Whether claiming promises during difficult times or citing verses to substantiate a view, make sure the texts you use to prove your point actually mean what you think they mean. Always be on the alert when reading books or listening to sermons. Are the authors or speakers simply quoting verses to buttress their points, or are they interpreting the Scripture carefully by looking at the details of the text?

Simply "claiming" a verse doesn't make it our own. Only when we are properly informed by God's Word the way it was written—in its context—can we be transformed by it. Every piece becomes powerful when it is working together according to the Spirit's design.

The sword of the Spirit is the Word of God (Ephesians 6:17). Used properly, it parries deception and pierces the heart. It protects us from error. A sword made of putty, though, has no power. It pierces nothing. It offers no protection. And it has no place in the arsenal of a Christian.

For Further Reading:

Gordon Fee & Douglas Stuart, *How to Read the Bible for All It's Worth* (Grand Rapids: Zondervan, 1982)

Walt Russell, *Playing with Fire—How the Bible Ignites Change in Your Soul* (Colorado Springs: NavPress, 2000)

James Sire, *Scripture Twisting* (Downers Grove: InterVarsity Press, 1980)

D.A. Carson, *Exegetical Fallacies* (Grand Rapids: Baker, 1984)

Endnotes

1. She would never say, for example, "The Holy Spirit gave me the fourth commandment." It's already hers.

2. It's not clear to me that Paul was making a promise even to the jailer other than if his family believed, they would be saved, too.

3. This is also the reason we do not "practice" at prophecy. Prophetic utterance is not an act of human will, so there's no skill at prophesying that needs to be developed.

4. Gordon Fee and Douglas Stuart, *How to Read the Bible for All Its Worth* (Grand Rapids: Zondervan, 1982), 27.

5. Of course, the Silly Putty method makes it impossible to imitate the virtuous Bereans. Since the meaning is not in the words, but in the mind of the reader, then "examining the Scriptures to see whether these things were so" will do them no good. No diligent study of the text will ever reveal what private message the Holy Spirit is giving to a reader. If it could, then the "Holy Spirit giveaway" would not have been necessary in the first place. The words of the text alone would have been sufficient.

6. Fee & Stuart, 26.

The Perils of Proof-Texting

Though reading Scripture is often a straightforward affair, there are pitfalls. Sometimes the "plain" meaning isn't so plain because it seems to conflict with another "plain" text that appears to say just the opposite. Now what?

The temptation is strong to simply pick the verse that seems to support our own pet theological view. If we're not careful, though, we'll end up pitting one biblical author against another, creating an apparent contradiction. This erodes the authority of the entire Bible.

In this essay, I want to show you how to avoid that danger. I give tips on how to resolve some of the apparent contradictions in Scripture. I've also included a detailed example on a controversial issue to give you a clear idea of how this works.

If you think you're on safe theological ground because of a pet verse, better look twice. Simple proof-texting has its perils. Here's how to avoid them.

Every Christian with a theological point of view thinks his view is scriptural. Why shouldn't he? He has a verse he can quickly quote in his defense.

This kind of "proof-texting" happens all the time on my radio show. A caller gives me his opinion, then cites his supporting verse. I can almost sense him settling back in his chair, folding his arms, and silently daring me to "disagree with God."

My verses say one thing, but his appear to say another. As long as he has a verse that—at least at first glance—seems to support his view, he's satisfied. Whenever the issue comes up, he simply quotes his pet text. His work is done, or so he thinks.

Creating Contradictions

Here's the problem. Countering the claim of one passage with a favorite verse for our own view might be satisfying for the moment because the verse affirms our pet doctrine. But the conflict created with other texts undermines the Bible's authority in general. When my verses say one thing and yours appear to say another, simply camping out on our proof-texts implicitly affirms a contradiction.

If there's a conflict, we must try to solve it. If we have a high view of Scripture—if we're convinced God would not contradict Himself in the Bible—then when something looks like a contradiction, we try to resolve it in a reasonable fashion. We try to find a legitimate way to harmonize passages that at first seem at odds with each other.

But how? First we ask if there's any possible flexibility or "wiggle room" in either of our proof-texts. We may be convinced of their meanings, but is it plausible to read the passages in a different way?

Next, we zoom out trying to get a wider picture by looking at other passages on the same topic. This allows us to factor in the whole counsel of God on the issue, gathering data from other passages hoping they will help break the tie between competing views. We do not simply ask, "What does *my verse* seem to say?" Rather, we try to consider *all* the relevant passages on the topic when we make our judgment.

This step entails the hardest task of all: giving genuine consideration to scriptural evidence that seems *contrary* to our own theology. How do we harmonize our view with the texts that seem against us to arrive at a coherent biblical expression of the issue?

One Voice or Many?

The very first step I take to resolve the problem of opposing verses is to explore the "flexibility" issue. Are the verses that have been cited *univocal* in what they declare, or *equivocal*. Let me explain what these words mean.

A univocal passage speaks with one voice ("uni-vocal") and is, therefore, unambiguous. When a text is univocal, it's hard to imagine any legitimate alternate meanings, even after looking at the passage from different angles.

Equivocal verses, on the other hand, have more than one plausible meaning. One interpretation may appear most obvious, but upon further study others suggest themselves.[1]

Noticing that the meaning of a certain verse or passage

may be equivocal is key to resolving the problem of apparent contradictions. Is it possible one or more of the proof-texts have more than one reasonable meaning? If so, then choosing one of the alternate meanings could remove the apparent contradiction. If one verse seems completely inflexible (univocal, or unequivocal), then adapt the more flexible verse (the equivocal one) to bring harmony.

Let me give you an example. Is baptism necessary for salvation? Is it necessary to be water baptized after one's profession of faith before one can receive the gift of forgiveness and new life through regeneration? Or is baptism a proper act of obedience *after* one becomes a Christian, but not necessary for salvation?

In the first case, the order would be faith, then baptism, resulting in salvation. In the second case the order would be faith, resulting in salvation, followed by baptism.

⚘ Peter vs. Peter

Verses seem to support both sides. In Acts 2:38 we read, "And Peter said to them, 'Repent, and let each of you be baptized in the name of Jesus Christ for the forgiveness of your sins, and you shall receive the gift of the Holy Spirit.'" If the repentant believer is baptized "*for* the forgiveness of sins," then repentance and belief are not enough. Baptism is needed to complete the sequence. The order in Acts 2 appears to be faith, then baptism, resulting in salvation.

This passage seems straightforward. To some, simply quoting it is enough. A problem arises, though, when we zoom out. When we read the record of the same apostle preaching the same message of salvation a few chapters later (Acts 10:44-48), we find this:

> While Peter was still speaking these words, the Holy Spirit fell upon all those who were listening to the message. And all the circumcised believers who had come with Peter were amazed, because the gift of the Holy Spirit had been poured out upon the gentiles also. For they were hearing them speaking with tongues and exalting God. Then Peter answered, "Surely no one can refuse the water for these to be baptized who have received the Holy Spirit just as we did, can he?" And he

ordered them to be baptized in the name of Jesus Christ. Then they asked him to stay on for a few days.

Notice what's happening. Peter—the same speaker as in Acts 2—preaches the Gospel to Cornelius and his household. In the midst of Peter's sermon, the Holy Spirit falls on those listening and they manifest spiritual gifts.

This is irrefutable evidence to Peter that these gentiles have "received the Holy Spirit just as [he] did." Other passages clearly state that possessing the Holy Spirit in the New Testament sense is proof of salvation (see Eph. 1:13-14 and Rom. 8:9).

After these gentiles are regenerated, Peter announces that water baptism is now appropriate. The order in Acts 10 is faith, resulting in salvation (the Spirit has already been given), followed by baptism.

The problem is obvious. Acts 2 seems to teach that salvation comes *after* water baptism, and Acts 10 indicates it can come *before* baptism. This appears to be a contradiction. Unless these passages are harmonized, merely asserting one verse against another actually does violence to the authority of God's Word.

This is when we must ask our question: Is either of the passages equivocal, that is, are there any legitimate alternative readings?

Here is my take. The Acts 10 passage seems completely inflexible in its meaning on the point at issue. It's univocal to me. The sequence of events leaves no question in my mind (though I'm open to suggestions) that this verse indicates faith and regeneration come before water baptism. Peter's own response seems to categorically eliminate alternate readings.

Further, when the Jewish leaders in the church later take issue with Peter about his involvement with gentiles, he simply recounts the event and they are satisfied (Acts 11:1-18). Note the wording:

If God, therefore, gave to them the same gift as He gave to us also after believing in the Lord Jesus Christ, who was I that I could stand in God's way?" And when they heard this, they quieted down, and glorified God, saying, "Well then, God has granted to the gentiles also the repentance that leads to life." (Acts 11:17-18)

Notice, baptism isn't even mentioned here, only the salient details of regeneration: repentance, faith, and salvation. By all appearances, Acts 10 is unambiguous. Water baptism is not necessary for salvation. Otherwise the sequence would have been different.

Which brings us back to Acts 2. The only hope for harmony is to find some flexibility in the wording here. Is it possible this passage is saying something different than it appeared to at first? On closer inspection I think the answer is, "Yes, it does." The key is in the grammar.

🦮 Guidance from Grammar

In Acts 2, the command to repent is in the plural in the Greek, as is the reference to those who receive the forgiveness of sins (i.e., "*All* of you repent so *all* of you can receive forgiveness"). The command to be baptized, however, is in the singular (i.e., "*Each* of you should be baptized").

Individual (singular) baptisms do not result in corporate (plural) salvations. The phrase "for the forgiveness of sins" then, does not modify baptism (as with the initial interpretation), but repentance. Repentance leads to salvation, not baptism. A more precise rendering might be, "Let all of you repent so all of you can receive forgiveness, and then each who has should be baptized."

Even if you're not completely convinced by this grammatical point alone regarding Acts 2:38, what I've offered is clearly a legitimate alternate reading. At bare minimum, then, when we look just at this one passage we have two interpretations finishing side by side.

Now Acts 10 and 11 come to our service to break the tie. Peter's gentiles are not getting baptized in order to *bring about* their salvation. They are baptized *as a result of* salvation. The clear (univocal) teaching in Acts 10 (and 11) helps us choose between the alternatives of the more ambiguous (equivocal) passage in Acts 2:38.

Not only is my take on the passage grammatically acceptable (even required, some would say), but it resolves the apparent contradiction, restoring harmony to God's Word.

My main point is this: to be balanced, our theological views should take into account the full body of scriptural references when considering an issue. Only then can we hope to clear up any apparent contradiction in the text.

Sometimes questions remain even when we're careful. Everything does not fall neatly into place. In times like these we do our best to lay our biases aside, look carefully at all the data, and then follow the evidence where it leads. The view that brings the most harmony between the relevant passages is probably going to be the right interpretation.

Doing Your Homework

Here's a tip on how to get that done with, say, the baptism issue.

Go to your Bible concordance and look up all the forms of the word "baptize" (e.g., "baptism" or "baptized"). Next write each reference on a 3x5 card or record it in a computer word processing file. Be sure to include the larger context of the verse if that seems to have any bearing on the meaning.

This step allows you to look at all the references together and begin to group them according to content. It will help you stay scripturally balanced, taking into account the full body of biblical references on an issue.

Many of the texts you'll find will be about John's baptism. Put them in one group. Others will be about the baptism of the Holy Spirit. Put those in another. There are references to the baptism of Moses and to baptism by fire. Jesus refers to yet another, the baptism of suffering ("Are you able to drink the cup that I drink, or to be baptized with the baptism with which I am baptized?" Mark 10:38).

Next, take the passages in each group one by one and look closely at what they say. Then begin drawing conclusions for the group based on the broad research—instead of proof-texting favorite verses—so you don't miss anything important. [2]

This is how to systematically study any doctrine or topic. The exercise takes a little time, but it can be a lot of fun and the results might even surprise you.[3] Doctrines begin to unfold before your eyes, giving you a solid biblical understanding on what might have previously been a muddled issue. By drawing instruction from the full counsel of God on a subject, you are able to make informed judgments that are biblically balanced.

You'll also notice that by surveying the full range of teaching in the New Testament on an issue (baptism, in this case) many distortions simply fade away.

When they don't, choose an interpretation that makes the best sense of all the relevant verses, especially if it legitimately harmonizes passages that at first seemed contradictory.

🏃 Honoring Inerrancy

This approach to resolving Bible conflicts takes biblical inerrancy for granted.[4] The Bible is the Word of God. God can't err. Therefore, the Bible can't err. When faced with apparent contradictions, then, we always look for a way to harmonize if possible. We do this by employing a core precept for understanding the Bible: Interpret the unclear in light of the clear.

If we have a high view of Scripture and are convinced God wouldn't contradict Himself, we will try to find a reasonable way to reconcile verses that seem to conflict. We do that by entertaining the possibility that our verse may have more than one possible meaning and, if so, by broadening our scope to see if other passages might help break the tie.

When all is said and done, there still may be problems. Though time and scholarship have resolved many, some still remain. At that point we acknowledge the difficulty and choose the view that in our opinion is best supported by the relevant passages. We try to remain open to better alternatives if they present themselves, and we always seek to be charitable with those who disagree.

🏃 Right Reading

Reading your Bible right—correctly—is a critical skill for ambassadors of Christ for a number of reasons. Let me give one of the most important. Contrary to what some believe, the words in the Bible have no power on their own. It's not enough to cite a verse, say the words, and expect something to happen. This is a superstitious—even occult—view of language (think "abracadabra").

No, there is no power in the words themselves, even when they are God's words. Only when God's words are used according to His meaning can we be transformed by them. Misconstruing a passage can actually neutralize the Word of God. It can rob the

Scripture of its authority and power. The entire reason we go to the Bible in the first place—to get God's truth and apply it to our lives—is thwarted.

Every verse becomes powerful only when used as the Holy Spirit intended. When we use a text the way God designed it to be used, then God Himself underwrites the promises and the teaching, releasing the power. If we take the Scripture in a way God did not mean it—if what we're getting *from* the verse is not really the teaching *of* the verse—then the words lose their authority.

As followers of Christ, our commitment should be to the truth of the passage, not to our pet doctrines. If we ignore that priority, then whatever confidence we may have will be based not on truth, but on fantasy.

Endnotes

1. As a rule, you never want to ground a significant theological point on an equivocal text. It's too easy for you to be mistaken.

2. Find examples of this on our web page at str.org. Search for "Principles of Successful Business from Proverbs," "Preaching God's Love in Acts?," or "The New Testament on Prayer."

3. In one study in Proverbs, for example, I learned that not all "bribes" were bad, only those that were used to pervert justice (17:23). Sometimes "a man's gift makes room for him and brings him before great men" (18:16), or a bribe "subdues... strong wrath" (21:14).

4. Establishing biblical inerrancy is a separate task.

Is the Bible Sufficient?

Controversy over the "adequacy" of the Bible has generated plenty of heat in Evangelical circles, particularly in the area of psychology. But are "Bible only" advocates right in claiming it's poison to combine man's philosophy with biblical wisdom to ease our emotional struggles?

Is this kind of thinking sound? More to the point, is it even biblical? Those are the questions I address in this essay.

What is it that makes an idea sound, legitimate, or worthwhile?

Let me put the question another way. If a point of view expressed by a Christian turns out to be correct, is the same notion any less legitimate when advanced by someone who is an unbeliever or even hostile to the Gospel?

By contrast, if a non-believer is wrong on some idea, does a bad notion become a good one if a Christian adopts it? Are believers right simply because they are spiritually regenerate, and non-believers consistently wrong merely because they are still in their sins?

What if that good belief, principle, or idea comes from the Bible? If God says it, you can count on it, of course. But what if a non-believer has the very same insight without the aid of special revelation? Is it still just as legitimate?

Further, what if a non-Christian weighs in with thoughts on things God has not given specific revelation on? Is it sound to simply dismiss his ideas because he is spiritually dead? Would the same notion in the mouth of a believer magically morph from deception to truth?

Here's why I'm asking these questions. Evangelicalism has been embroiled for some time in a controversy of no small proportion. Authors we have trusted for years, whose counsel has elevated our Christian experience and deepened our understanding of ourselves and of God, have been branded heretics in some circles.

Why have these men been vilified? Because they employ principles gleaned from psychology and not specifically from the Bible, thus—according to detractors—producing a poisonous amalgam of biblical wisdom and godless philosophy.

The Bible is fully sufficient, say critics. "The Word of God has been given to man as the *sole* source for finding God's solutions to the real problems that plague him." They decry "futile attempts to mix God's Word with *unregenerate suppositions and theories.*" [1] [emphasis mine]

An important part of being a thoughtful Christian is growing in the ability to winnow wheat from chaff, separating facts from falsehoods. Part of that skill depends on knowing how to distinguish good reasons from bad ones. Answering the question of the Bible's adequacy requires that skill, but the task is compromised when right-hearted and well-intentioned people try to resolve the issue in a wrong-headed way.

Many have a deep suspicion of solutions addressing the human condition—especially in the area of psychology—that have been developed by those who are not taking their cues from the counsel in God's Word.

Their misgivings are justified in many cases. But some go further and disqualify *all* such reflections out of hand as tainted at their source by spiritual blindness, darkened understanding, and rebellion.

It's hard to argue with the noble desire to focus on training materials that are more directly biblical. And it's also possible that respected leaders in our midst can do us harm. Wolves come in sheep's clothing, after all.

Sometimes, though, the distinction between fleece and fur is not so easily determined and good men are vilified without cause. Proof texts used to condemn them may seem crystal clear at first, but take on a different sense when examined more closely or when balanced against other scriptural teaching.

I won't comment here on the role of psychology in the life of the Christian except to say I'm a centrist on the issue. I'm concerned here with a more foundational idea: Is the Bible "sufficient" in the sense that these critics claim?

✒ Scripture on the "Adequacy" of Scripture

Advocates rely on a handful of references to show that Scripture provides the sole solutions to life's problems. These three are characteristic:

- "You shall not add to the word which I am commanding you, nor take away from it, that you may keep the commandments of the Lord your God which I command you" (Deut. 4:2).

- "Do not add to His words lest He reprove you, and you be proved a liar" (Prov. 30:6).

- "And if anyone takes away from the words of the book of this prophecy, God shall take away his part from the tree of life and from the holy city, which are written in this book" (Rev. 22:19).

Verses used to prove the "Bible only" view must be considered in their context, though. On closer inspection, none of these passages teach what is claimed. The Deuteronomy reference only prohibits changing the specific revelation that Moses has just given. Note that 61 additional books of the Bible were written after Moses penned these lines in the Pentateuch. Further, the passage does not forbid the use of man's observations about life and human behavior.

The Proverbs passage simply says not to add to God's Word. No Christian I'm aware of, though, considers principles of psychology or philosophy equal to Scripture in authority.

Rev. 22:19 forbids adding to the "words of the book of this prophecy," that is, that specific revelation itself. This verse is not even limiting the extent of the canon, much less excluding human wisdom about man's problems.

Another passage however, 2 Tim. 3:16-17, is more substantial.

✒ 2 Timothy 3:16-17

Paul writes in his last epistle, "All Scripture is inspired by God and profitable for teaching, for reproof, for correction, for training in righteousness, that the man of God may be adequate, equipped for every good work."

The reasoning on this passage by "Bible only" advocates goes something like this. Paul says that Scripture is adequate. If

Scripture is adequate, then nothing more is required. If nothing more is required, then the use of outside material implies the inadequacy of the Bible, contradicting Paul's statement. Therefore, nothing in addition to Scripture can be used to equip us, because nothing else is "profitable for teaching, for reproof, for correction, for training in righteousness." This function is the sole province of the Bible.

That's the argument. Here's what's wrong with it.

First, 2 Timothy 3:15 does not teach that Scripture is "adequate." Look closely at the grammar. The word "adequate" modifies the *believer*, not the *Scripture*, "the man of God" who uses the inspired Scripture in a profitable way. The words Paul uses to describe Scripture are "inspired" and "profitable," not "adequate." The Bible, then, is useful to accomplish a certain end—an adequately equipped Christian—because it is the very counsel of God. Paul's teaching in 2 Timothy was meant to *qualify* the nature of Scripture, not to *disqualify* the usefulness of other material.

What does "adequate" mean here? It probably means what adequate usually means, that the man of God has everything that is essential. Food and air and water are adequate to keep one alive, but their adequacy doesn't imply that nothing else is beneficial.

Second, the argument proves too much. The Scripture Paul has in view are the sacred writings of Timothy's childhood (note verse 15), the Old Testament. These are what Paul identifies as being able to "give you the wisdom that leads to salvation through faith which is in Christ Jesus."

If the Old Testament scriptures are adequate in the sense that "Bible only" folks mean—if Paul means to teach that the addition of any outside information about man and his condition implies the inadequacy of Scripture—then how do we justify adding the words of the New Testament to the fully adequate Old Testament? Even Paul's words (as well as Peter's, John's, and the rest) would be inadmissible, including the very words of 2 Tim. 3:16-17 that make this claim.

The argument as it stands, then, is self-defeating. It commits suicide and the entire objection crumbles. Therefore, Paul did not mean to convey that other sources of knowledge were an assault on the Scripture's completeness.

Some have pointed out that my argument could be used to teach that Paul thought only the Old Testament was inspired, not the New. Not so. Paul's statement was about Scripture in general—the authoritative writings—which at that time was what we now call the Old Testament. He did not say that no more "God-breathed" writings would be forthcoming. The corpus of Scripture was expanded by the New Testament writers and therefore it is included under the claims of this verse.

The problem only arises if one imposes a foreign sense of adequacy on this passage, i.e., nothing else is allowed. My point is that if Paul and the Apostles wrote legitimate Scripture after the Old Testament period, this proves that in this passage Paul did not intend his statement to impose the restrictions the "Bible only" advocates imagine.

But there are other problems with the "Bible only" view.

🐾 Proverbs and Wisdom from Nature

Scripture itself seems to encourage us to take counsel from extra-biblical sources of information. In Genesis, for example, God gave a command, but gave no details of how to accomplish it. The mandate to be fruitful and multiply cannot be fulfilled without the ability of man to observe his environment, learn useful things, and then employ them to improve his condition—all apart from special revelation, since most men do not possess it.

This is precisely what we find in the book of Proverbs. According to Solomon, wise counselors are those who are skilled at life, including the ability to observe the natural realm and deduce spiritual truth, moral knowledge, and skills at living.

Note this statement in Proverbs 24:30-34:

> I passed by the field of the sluggard, and by the vineyard of the man lacking sense, and behold, it was completely overgrown with thistles. Its surface was covered with nettles, and its stone wall was broken down. When I saw, *I reflected upon it. I looked, and received instruction.* "A little sleep, a little slumber, a little folding of the hands to rest," then your poverty will come as a robber, and your want like an armed man.

Proverbs shows that we can draw true conclusions about right conduct from astute observations about the world. Even before the sage says, "My son, observe the commandment of your father" (6:20), he says, "Go to the ant, O sluggard. Observe *her* ways and be wise" (5:6).

In other words, God reveals Himself in propositional form (Scripture) and non-propositional form (nature). Through observation and reflection on either—if they are properly interpreted—one can infer principles for living because *both* inform man how to live well.

Taking his own advice, the sage of Proverbs makes this observation:

> *Four things are small on the earth, but they are exceedingly wise. The ants are not a strong folk, but they prepare their food in the summer. The badgers are not mighty folk, yet they make their houses in the rocks. The locusts have no king, yet all of them go out in ranks. The lizard you may grasp with the hands, yet it is in kings' palaces (30:24-28).*

Consider this scenario. When a city is plagued by violence, the people decide to execute murderers. Immediately the murder rate drops and peace is restored to the city. These people used their fallen, human wisdom to employ a biblical solution—government bearing the sword to mitigate the impact of evil (Rom. 13:4). They accurately assess and solve a human problem, even without knowledge of Scripture. This kind of thing happens all the time.

Wisdom from the Heathen

The *Wisdom Literature of the Amenomope* is a body of work from the Middle East that pre-dates Proverbs. It's of interest because it contains a section of material almost identical to Proverbs 22:17-24:22. It's highly probable that the authors of the latter part of Proverbs borrowed this material from the *Amenomope* and inserted it into the inspired text.

Some scholars see this as a serious compromise of the doctrine of inspiration. However, a more biblical view removes the objection. Clearly, natural man apart from God is capable of discerning truth that, according to its appearance in Proverbs, is from God.

Paul's classic teaching in Romans 1:18ff identifies the universal, innate ability of man to draw conclusions about God's nature without the aid of special revelation—a capability so effective that the willful suppression of it brings God's judgment.

Keep in mind that the specific details Paul identifies here—"His invisible attributes, His eternal power and divine nature"—are only *examples* of natural revelation, not the total *sum* of it. He doesn't limit our knowledge to only basic information about God's existence.

In Gen. 18:25, Abraham challenges God's plan to destroy Sodom and Gomorrah: "Far be it from You to do such a thing, to slay the righteous with the wicked, so that the righteous and the wicked are treated alike. Far be it from You! Shall not the Judge of all the earth deal *justly*?"

This is a striking challenge since Abraham's question comes 400 years before the Law was given. Where did Abraham get his notion of justice? Clearly, it was innate, part of God's natural revelation to all men. It did not have to be discovered in Scripture. It was part of the moral law already written on his heart (Rom. 2:14-15).

✾ Knowledge from Natural Revelation

One thing at stake in this discussion is the legitimacy of natural theology, that which can be known about God and about man's spiritual condition through general revelation—broadly, through reasoning and personal experience. Can unregenerate man know anything significant, especially in the spiritual realm, without the aid of special revelation? The Bible seems to teach he can know much.

Francis Schaeffer pointed out that the Bible is "true truth," but not exhaustive truth. It is completely true about everything to which it speaks, but it doesn't speak about everything there is to know. Much more can be discovered.

Bruce Demarest, Professor of Systematic Theology at Denver Seminary, makes this observation:

> *God wills that man, the pinnacle of His creation, should use his reason to secure truth, including elementary truths about himself. Equipped with an intuitional knowledge of God, including the light of conscience, and*

*enabled by common grace, man by rational reflection
on the data of the natural and historical order draws
inferences about God's character and operations.*[2]

Man made in the image of God gains knowledge from general revelation. He has an innate ability to know first principles and basic rules of logic, Demarest argues, and knows how to apply these abilities to learn truth, not just about his world, but also—in a limited way—about the spiritual realm.

Demarest concludes, "Scripture supports our thesis that further truth content about God is acquired by rational reflection on God's general revelation on nature in history."[3]

A case in point is Dr. Bernard Nathanson, one of the founders of the National Abortion Rights Action League (NARAL). For years, Nathanson ran one of the largest commercial abortion operations in the country. He later repudiated the practice and became an ardent advocate of the rights of the unborn child.

Why the change of heart? Because Nathanson became convinced that abortion was a serious violation of human dignity. The irony is that Bernard Nathanson made this about-face as an atheist (though he later converted to Catholicism).

One could argue it's very hard to justify the concept of human rights—a type of transcendent law—if there is no God to serve as the transcendent source of law. Nathanson's reversal, however, proves it's possible for those with faulty philosophical foundations to reason *inconsistently* to a conclusion that turns out to be true.

Nathanson's thinking was inconsistent with his world view, but his intuitive knowledge of human value—a function of general revelation—was correct. And if this is possible for Nathanson the atheist, wouldn't it also be possible for others like him (Freud or Maslow or Jung) who, though fallen and unregenerate, are still made in the image of God?

The View of the Reformers

Even the Reformers, aggressive in asserting "total depravity"[4] and advocates of *sola scriptura*, did not hold to the radical version of "Bible only" in question here. Note Calvin:

*In reading profane authors, the admirable light of truth
displayed in them should remind us that the human*

mind, however much fallen and perverted from its original integrity, is still adorned and invested with admirable gifts from its Creator....Their example should teach us how many gifts the Lord has left in possession of human nature, not withstanding of its having been despoiled of the true good.[5]

Calvin does not take lightly this "despoiling." Regarding spiritual discernment—"the knowledge of God, the knowledge of...our salvation and the method of regulating our conduct in accordance with the Divine Law"—he says that "the mind of man must ever remain a mere chaos of confusion. To the great truths, what God is in Himself, and what He is in relation to us, human reason makes not the least approach."[6]

Calvin distinguishes between two kinds of knowledge. He calls them natural gifts and supernatural gifts. Calvin holds, with Augustine, that man's natural gifts were corrupted by sin, but not withdrawn.[7] He then continues for almost five pages in his *Institutes* detailing the capabilities of fallen reason.

According to Calvin, only man's supernatural gifts were lost, specifically "the light of faith and righteousness, which would have been sufficient for the attainment of heavenly life and everlasting felicity."[8]

Would this great Reformer categorically condemn the contributions of modern psychology as mere worldly wisdom? I don't think so. Calvin even extols what he calls the "shrewd" observations of Aristotle: that people have a tendency to acknowledge general moral principles, but go into denial when they personally contemplate committing sin. Afterwards, guilt and remorse set in.[9]

Whether or not one agrees with Calvin's particular application here is incidental to my point. What is important is that John Calvin—a principal Reformer with a robust understanding of man's fallenness and a deep commitment to the authority of God's Word—quotes an unregenerate Greek philosopher reflecting on the vicissitudes of the human psyche. *Calvin is using Aristotle's psychology to help articulate an aspect of man's fallenness.*

🏃 Adequacy

The question "Is Scripture adequate?" is much like the question "Is Christ adequate?" The answer depends entirely upon what one expects either to do. Each one does something specific for us; neither does everything. In one sense, God wasn't even adequate for Adam in the garden. Though Adam was walking in unfallen fellowship with the Father, God still said, "It is not good for the man to be alone. I will make him a helper suitable for him" (Gen. 2:18).

The Bible is sufficient to give the "wisdom that leads to salvation" and to enable the godly person to be "adequate, equipped for every good work" (2 Tim. 3:15, 17), no question. Such sufficiency, however, does not preclude other sources of learning that give further instruction in mental health and skill at living when winnowed by the truth already given in God's Word.

Scripture, general revelation, history, and our own experience all bear witness to the fact that man has a God-given ability to discover useful truth and make accurate and useful assessments about life and its problems.

The Scripture is the standard of truth to be studied, applied, and cherished. The Bible itself, however, doesn't support the "Bible only" view. It does not teach that man is so distorted by sin as to lose his ability to discover useful truth on his own, even some "spiritual" truth. It teaches, rather, that man has an extensive ability to draw from general revelation to make accurate and useful assessments about life, its vexing problems, and even some of its solutions.

Christians who promote the narrow "Bible only" view, however well-intentioned, encourage unnecessary conflict in the church. They also deny believers a source of wisdom and knowledge from general revelation that the Bible itself encourages us to discover and benefit from.

Endnotes

1. John C. Broger, *Self-Confrontation* syllabus (Rancho Mirage, CA: Biblical Counseling Foundation, 1991). It's not entirely clear to me what "unregenerate suppositions and theories" are, because ideas and theories aren't the subjects of regeneration; people are. Possibly he meant those suppositions or theories coming from unregenerate people.

2. Bruce Demarest, *General Revelation: Historical Views and Contemporary Issues* (Zondervan: Grand Rapids, 1982), 233.

3. Ibid., 234.

4. "Total depravity" is the accepted term, but I've put it in quotes because it's actually a misnomer, giving the mistaken impression that man is incapable of producing anything good or of value. Our term "total depravity" actually means that no part of man is untouched and untainted by the fall. The *extent* of the impact of the fall is total, not the *degree*.

5. *Institutes*, Book II, ch. 2, para. 15.

6. Ibid., para. 18.

7. Ibid., para. 12.

8. Ibid.

9. Ibid., para. 23.

Four for the Road

I close Ancient Words with four brief vignettes. Each is too short for an entire chapter, but all are important, so I gathered them together here. Every section touches on an important issue related to the proper use of God's Word. I hope you find these to be prime, practical resources for your own personal study of the greatest book ever written.

Biblical Fast Food?

I suspect my schedule is much like yours—hectic. When time is tight it's tempting to take a "fast food" approach to the Bible—grabbing something quick and eating it on the run. Like many Christians, I've had stretches when small bites were my standard diet. There were other seasons, though, when I made it a point to sit down regularly and take time for a civilized meal.

During one spring, for example, I worked my way through the entire Old Testament as part of a class assignment. In order to keep up my Bible reading, it was first on my agenda each morning, and I had to read ten pages a day.

Two things stood out about this exercise. First, *I found the time*, in spite of my other obligations. I had no choice. I had to finish the class, so I made it happen.

Second, *I enjoyed the meal*. I had a sense of being nourished because I was experiencing the Scripture the way the Holy Spirit gave it: in unified accounts—discussions with flow, context, order, and purpose. Entire passages came alive in ways the fast food approach could never accomplish.

This raises a question concerning the daily devotionals that are so popular today, handbooks of short messages built around single verses, sometimes just phrases. For many, these vignettes have become their primary source of daily nourishment. They're inspirational and they're quick, able to be wedged into the busiest schedule. But they come with a dangerous drawback.

By focusing only on pieces of a passage, we may actually miss the author's point of the verse. If we're just reading snatches of text, what's our guarantee the inspirational feelings we experience aren't just false hopes or mere emotion? The difference is critical. It's the distinction between believe and make-believe.

As Christians, our commitment should be to the truth of the passage, not to the feeling a certain reading of that passage gives us. If we ignore that priority, then whatever sense of satisfaction we enjoy from our quick meal might have been based on fantasy. [1]

If you habitually take the fast food approach when it comes to the Bible, try this experiment. For three months, put away your one-verse devotionals. Instead, *make* the time to sit down with the Lord to a real meal. Don't be satisfied with tidbits. Commit yourself to reading whole chapters.

I suspect that if you do this, you will quickly begin to notice the difference as you "renew your mind" each day. You'll be confident that the sense of comfort and safety you experience will be grounded in truth and not presumption, fact and not fantasy.

You may even find you'll never go back to biblical "fast food" again.

Taking the Bible "Literally"—Part I

I never like the question, "Do you take the Bible literally?" It comes up with some frequency, and it deserves a response, but I think it's a confusing and ambiguous query. This makes it awkward to answer.

Clearly, even those with a high view of Scripture don't take *everything* literally. Jesus is the "door," but He's not made of wood. We are the "branches," but we're not sprouting leaves.

On the other hand, we *do* take seriously accounts others find fanciful and far-fetched: a man made from mud (Adam), loaves and fishes miraculously multiplied, corpses walking out of graves, etc.

A short "yes" or "no" response to the "Do you take the Bible literally?" question, then, would not be helpful. Neither answer gives the right impression.

I'd like to suggest an alternative response that might lead to a productive conversation. Here it is: "I take the Bible in its *ordinary* sense."

I realize this reply is also a bit ambiguous, but here, I think, that's a strength. Hopefully, your answer will prompt a request for clarification. This is exactly what you want, as long as *you* are clear in your own mind what you mean.

I would clarify what *I* have in mind by countering with another question. When someone asks for an explanation of my comment, I ask, "Do you read the *sports page* literally?"

I think this question would give anyone pause. Certain factual information is part of every story in that section. On the other hand, no one would be tempted to think that a football team was *literally* "crushed," "mangled," "mutilated," "pounded," "stomped," "shredded," or "devoured."

"*Literally*?" they might respond. "That depends. If the writer seems to be stating a fact—like a score, a location, a player's name, a description of the plays leading to a touchdown—then I'd take that as fact. If he seems to be using a figure of speech, then I'd take his statement less literally."

This is a good response. It's the normal way to read the sports page. It's also the normal way of reading any work, including the Bible. And this is exactly what I mean when I say, "I take the Bible in its ordinary sense." When a writer seems to be communicating facts in a straight-forward fashion, I read them as such. When I encounter obvious figures of speech, I take them that way, too.

Even figurative speech—in prose at least—is meant to communicate literal truth in a more precise and powerful way than ordinary language would be able to do. Figures are always meant to *clarify*, not *obscure*. So even if you don't take a particular phrase "literally," some literal point is still being made. That's why it's always right to ask, "What is the *precise message* the writer is trying to communicate with his colorful language?"

Let's face it, even non-Christians read the Bible in its ordinary sense most of the time. No one denies we should take at face value statements like "love your neighbor" or "remember the poor." They only abandon the "literal" approach when they come across something in the account that's inconsistent with their own theological or moral sensibilities. Then, suddenly, they become skeptics and sniff, "You don't take the Bible *literally*, do you?"

When this happens, tell them you take the words with the

precision you think the original author intended. If they disagree, ask them for the reasons they think their passage should be an exception to an otherwise sound rule. Their answer will tell you if their challenge is intellectually honest, or if they are trying to dismiss biblical claims they simply don't like.

Do I take the Bible literally? Well, I try to I take it at its plain meaning unless I have some good reason to do otherwise. This is the basic rule we apply to everything we read: novels, newspapers, periodicals, and poems. I don't see why the Bible should be any different.

Taking the Bible "Literally"—II

In my first reflection I warned about the liability of simply answering yes to the question "Do you take the Bible literally?" Rather, I suggested, you could avoid confusion by saying, "I take the Bible in its *ordinary* sense."

Maybe you've encountered another challenge in the "taking the Bible literally" category. Here's one example I was confronted with.

In the Law of Moses, homosexual activity was punishable by death (Leviticus 18:22-23 and 20:13). Therefore (the charge goes), any Christian who takes the Bible literally must advocate the execution of homosexuals. If he doesn't, then he is not taking the Bible literally, and no one else should, either.

Let's start with a definition. According to the *New Oxford American Dictionary*, the word "literal" means, "Taking words in their usual or most basic sense without metaphor or allegory, free from exaggeration or distortion."

Now here's our question: When Moses wrote the Law, did he expect the Jewish people to take those regulations literally?

If the question gives you pause, let me ask it another way. When an ordinance is passed in your local state (California, in my case), do you think the legislators intend that you understand the words of the regulation "in their usual or most basic sense without metaphor or allegory, free from exaggeration or distortion?"

Of course they do. Legal codes are not written in figurative language allowing each citizen to get creative with the meaning. The same would be true for the Mosaic Law. Moses meant it the way he wrote it.

But now, it seems, we're stuck on the other horn of the dilemma. To be consistent, shouldn't we currently campaign for the death penalty for homosexuals? For that matter, aren't we obliged to promote execution for disobedient children and Sabbath-breakers, both capital crimes under the Law?

The simple answer is no. Here's why. Just because a biblical command is intended to be understood *literally*, does not mean it is intended to be applied *universally*.

Consider this situation. Jesus told Peter to cast his net in deep water (Luke 5:4). That's exactly what Peter did because he took Jesus' command literally, in its ordinary sense. He had no reason to think otherwise. However, because Jesus' command to Peter was literal does not mean the same command applies to us. *We're* not obliged to cast nets into deep water just because Peter was.

Here's another way of looking at it. No matter what state you live in, the California legal codes are to be *read* literally. But they don't *apply* to you unless you actually live in California. In the same way, the words of the Mosaic Law, like those of all laws, are to be taken at face value by anyone who reads it. Yet only those under its jurisdiction are obliged to obey it.

The Jews in the theocracy were expected to obey the legal code God gave them. It was not the legal code God gave to gentiles, however. Therefore, even if the words of the Mosaic Law are to be taken literally, this does not mean that in our current circumstances we are governed by every detail of the provisions of that Law.

The real question we face is not whether we *take* the Mosaic Law literally, but whether we are now *under* that legal code. We are not. That law was meant for Jews living under the theocracy of the Mosaic Covenant. Americans are a mixture of peoples in a representative republic governed by a different decree.

Though we may glean wisdom and moral guidance from the Law of Moses for our own legal codes, we are not obliged to obey everything that came down from Sinai. Just because it was commanded of the Jews does not mean it is commanded of us.[2] If anyone thinks otherwise, he is duty-bound to take his net and cast it into deep water.

🐟 Promises, Promises

When I was a new believer in the 70s, part of the standard

"gear" for Jesus Movement Christians was a dog-eared paperback copy of *The Jesus Person Pocket Promise Book.*

It seemed like a sensational idea at the time: Collect God's promises, then cash them in as needed. Now, nearly 40 years later—though the promises of God are no less "precious and magnificent" (2 Peter 1:4)—I think twice when I hear people claim them.

For one, promises are frequently abused, sometimes by people who should know better. A promise not carefully tethered to the details of the text becomes an empty exercise in relativistic wishful thinking.

Second, knowledge—"an accurately informed mind"—is the first characteristic of a good ambassador. Ambassadors need to be right on the meaning of a biblical message before they can safely pass it on to others. Since everything we offer others on God's behalf consists of promises of some sort, mistakes here really matter.

A biblical promise is a binding pledge from God to do—or not do—something specific. If the promise is made to you, you have a right to expect God will keep His word. If you are not the rightful owner of the promise, though, you may not lay claim to it. It is theft to try to cash in on promises made to someone else.

But how do you know if you are the fortunate beneficiary? You find out by looking closely at the details of the promise itself and applying two simple principles.

First, the correct meaning of any biblical passage is the meaning the author had in mind when he wrote it. A promise is only a promise when it is used as its maker intended. Second, we discover the author's intent by paying attention to the specifics, the details that make up the meat of the promise—the words, the conditions, the recipient, the timing, and the historical setting.

The process can be organized into steps by asking (and answering) four questions: Who? What? Why? and When?[3]

Who?—Identify the particular person or group the promise is made to. The promise may be for a specific individual, or for a particular group, or for anyone at all. Ask yourself, "Am I that person?" If the promise is to a group (e.g. Jews, Christians) ask, "Am I part of that group?"

What?—Zero in on the particulars of the promise. Specify what the promise actually commits to. Ask, "What will happen (or not happen) when the promise is fulfilled?"

Why?—Note the conditions or requirements the promise hinges on, often signaled by an "if/then" clause—e.g., "*If* you continue in My word, *then* you are truly disciples of Mine and you will know the truth, and the truth will make you free" (John 8:31-32). Ask, "Do I meet the requirements?"

When?—Determine the time for the fulfillment of the promise. It may be for a particular point in the future ("…at this time next year …") or for an unspecified time. Ask the question "What is the time of the promise, if any?"

Be sure to get your answers to these questions by looking carefully at the words of the promise itself in light of the larger context of the passage. Keep in mind you may have to read an entire chapter or more to gather enough information to answer your questions.

Now, a short homework assignment. Here is a list of popular promises. Grab a sheet of paper and apply our four questions to each one and see what you come up with. This will be fun or painful, depending on how you've read these promises in the past.

> *John 1:12; John 3:18; Romans 8:28* (note 29-30); *Joshua 1:9* (note 1:1-9); *2 Chronicles 7:14* (the full context starts in chapter 6. Make note of the details of Solomon's prayer in 6:17-27 in light of God's specific response to him in the next chapter.)

We can only legitimately lay hold of a Bible promise if it's rightfully ours. When we claim promises belonging to someone else, the appeal falls on deaf ears. God does not honor claims we make on promises He has actually made to others and not to us.

However, if the promise is for us—if we're the ones the promise is directed to, if we have satisfied the conditions, and if the promise is for our time—then we can count on God to follow through on our behalf.

If not, then we must leave the promise to its rightful owner and profit from the text by learning what we can from God's faithful dealings with them.

Endnotes

1. A notable exception to this trend is *Our Daily Bread*, a publication of Radio Bible Class Ministries (rbc.org). Their devotions consistently focus on a paragraph or more—sometimes an entire chapter—not just one verse. I have rarely seen them wrench a text out of context to make a devotional point.

2. I am not claiming there is *nothing* in the Law that has application for us or that there are *no* universal moral obligations we share with the Jews of Moses' time. That is a different discussion. I am merely saying that simply because a directive appears in the Mosaic Law does not, by that fact alone, make it obligatory upon those living outside of Israel's theocracy.

3. I am indebted to my brother, David Koukl, for the insights in this section, and for this useful exercise.